HEART AWAKENING:

Your Path to

Unconditional Love & Healing

by

Raoult Bertrand

Michaela,
Divine Light
Divine Love
Divine Peace
and so on

Raoult
Bertrand

Consciousness of Light
P.O. Box 4195
Cave Creek, Arizona, 85327
United States of America
Phone: 800-370-5479 or 480-488-1731
Fax: 480-488-5806
Email: contact@ConsciousnessofLight.com
Web site: www.ConsciousnessofLight.com

Author's note: The stories in this book are true, however names, locations and other identifying information have been changed or omitted to protect confidentiality. Due to federal trademark issues, the web
site address has changed (HeartAwakening.com),
although it is the original healing work practiced by
Raoult Bertrand since 1987.

Publisher and Editor
Shari Jo Sorchych
Interior and Cover Design
Gena Maynard

ISBN 978-0-615-18921-5

DEDICATION

To Spirit,
my guides, my teachers,
and all those who have the
courage to accept a Heart
Awakened world as
living truth

May your willingness
to love all, and to serve all
set your soul
eternally
free.

Acknowledgements

To all those who have ever had or intend to have a Heart Awakening session or participated in the gatherings and the workshops, I extend my deepest gratitude and appreciation. The opportunity to serve you is an incredible source of inspiration for me. Through you, I have been continually challenged to actualize the potential of what I can become. You are making my vision of a Heart Awakened world a living reality and you provided me with an endless memory of life-transforming Heart Awakening experiences, the richness of which will feed my soul forever. Words will never convey how much I am nourished by what we are sharing together.

To all the Heart Awaking practitioners, please know I am deeply grateful for your undying loyalty and support since my teaching journey began. Your dedication and efforts have made it possible to reach so many more.

To the editors who have helped, I extend my thanks for their many hours of diligent work in transcribing and editing this book, and for the patience and perseverance necessary to bring congruency, order, and flow to this written text.

To Rosemary Wilkie, my mother, whose selfless, untiring dedication to me and to Heart Awakening gives me the strength to continue when life's challenges are the greatest, I send my love and gratitude.

To all my family members, including my father Maxime's family, and my brother Guy and his family, I acknowledge your presence with me on my journey.

To the late Ron Hall, who reoriented my life onto

the spiritual healing path and whose great wisdom served as the initial inspiration for Heart Awakening, I am most appreciative.

To Wauneta Beeler, my deceased partner who helped my transition from the entrepreneurial life to a world of healing, I am forever indebted. Her love and dedication helped me develop this work. She taught me compassion, selfless service, and the difference between personal love and Divine Love.

To all those others who have received the truth of this work and provided me with continual understanding of Spirit's eternal presence and the perfection of the unfolding of this work, I humbly thank you.

Last but not least, to all the faculty and students at the school, I am grateful for their gifts of revealing themselves and demonstrating their faith in the vision of Heart Awakening.

FOREWORD

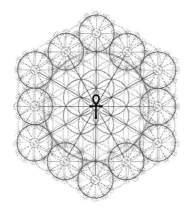

Heart Awakening:

To our culture…

A vision of our future without pain or regret.

By "a soul that knew"

The quality of the healing work defined as Heart Awakening comes through silent prayer and meditation on the One Divine Source as well as study with numerous healers and teachers of the spiritual healing arts.

The author and other practitioners of Heart Awakening are not medical doctors nor license physicians nor licensed psychologists nor licensed psychotherapists. Persons with psychological or physical illness that require a medical doctor or psychologist or psychotherapist should contact licensed practitioners. Heart Awakening is different in that it is a method of working with energies of consciousness only. The author and other Heart Awakening practitioners do not recommend the discontinuance of legend drugs or controlled substances prescribed by an appropriately licensed practitioner. Heart Awakening is an alternative or complementary to traditional healing services licensed by the State of Arizona.

Heart Awakening spiritual healing works with nonphysical body energies, and thus may be unproven according to the FDA and AMA. Therefore, no claims can be made or are made for its effectiveness or use for treating psychiatric or physical health problems. Heart Awakening is not intended to be a substitute for appropriate medical care by a licensed physician. Terminology used by the author, or his assistants, or representatives, or other Heart Awakening practitioners in no way corresponds to medically labeled psychological or physical ailments, diseases, dysfunctions, or physical phenomena; terminology used only serves as labels for various kinds of nonphysical energy health. Heart Awakening as an occupation has been applied for with the U.S. Department of Labor. Heart Awakening services are of a nonphysical energy and educational nature, only. Heart Awakening services are based upon the theory that nonphysical energy is the basis of reality and that by working with nonphysical energy, reality can be improved.

The education, training, experience, and other qualifications of the author/practitioner of Heart Awakening services consist of: study in the healing art of Awakening, Shamanism, Kabbalah, Gigong, Keys of Enoch, Jin Shin Jyutsu, Yoga, Tibetan, Buddhism, Egyptian Mystery Teachings, Aura and Chakra Healing, Internal Release of Disinformation, nutrition, silent meditation, and several thousand hours of one on one or group healing work, a healing school and numerous new teachings that are unique to the new wave of spiritual energies present in the southwestern area of the U.S.

The author and other Heart Awakening practitioners are spiritual healers and all healing that occurs with their work comes from The One Divine Source, recognized by each religion in its own way – God, Source, the Indwelling Presence, Nature, Christ, etc. Considering the source of the healing, the reader is invited to give responsibility for the outcome of this material to The One Divine Source.

Raoult Bertrand,
Founder
Cave Creek, Arizona

The Gift of Heart Awakening

The primary purpose of Heart Awakening sessions is to help people open their hearts. The single most important need for mankind at this time is to learn how to shift out of our everyday problems and fully experience Divine Love within ourselves. There is a single heartbeat deep within each and every one of us which pulses at the resonant frequency of Divine Love. Each time we give from our hearts, this Divine force is released a little more. Pain turns to joy and fear turns to love; appreciation, abundance, and true happiness are realized.

Opening our hearts is probably what we need most but have developed the greatest skill for resisting and deferring. We think nothing of improving ourselves by getting our hair done, buying new clothes, getting a massage, or changing our ideas, but what of our hearts? What of the Divine Love that should forever be felt as a part of our daily lives? How many times have we looked into ourselves, felt what we didn't like to feel, and avoided dealing with issues of the heart by reverting to the intellect or by denying the issues altogether?

True living begins with an open heart. True living is having compassion for self and others, accepting ourselves and others just as we were created in our Divine image, and knowing nothing is more important than the Love. Once we have experienced and accepted the eternalness of the deep, indwelling Divine Love, we can open the door to honest relationships with others and share the wisdom born of spiritual Love with anyone, anywhere, at any time.

Within the expression of Divine Love is a Divine plan for the restoration of peace on earth. This plan reveals itself everywhere we go, within everything we do, and within everyone we meet. Heart Awakening is the process of becoming conscious of that plan and actively participating in its unfoldment. This occurs the moment we open our hearts and feel the Love within.

When we step into the new world of unconditional love, we discover the bridge that converts poverty into abundance and transforms isolation into unity among friends and family. An open heart is a gift. It is available all the time, under any circumstances. The question to ask ourselves is, "How can I be in that space here and now?"

Have you ever felt as if you were drifting from one day to the next hoping to get by, not really able to do much, because you have lost your direction and purpose? Most of us have grown numb, not recognizing the extent to which we have drifted away from actualizing our soul's potential. The heart is the gateway to the soul, so ask yourself, "What has happened to my heart?" Only when this question is asked in earnest can the true quest for your soul's journey begin.

Heart Awakening is a way to rediscover your true essence and is available to those of us who genuinely want to know the next step of our soul's journey. It is for everyone yearning to embrace and deepen their experience of the Divine. It is an exploration in consciousness where we can reach any level for which we are ready, a vehicle through which we can participate in the earth's current transformation by informing ourselves experientially of who and what we are when our hearts are opened. Forever. An awakened heart is only available to us when we're willing to come into full integrity in all areas of our lives, no matter what the outer circumstances may be.

There may be other ways to open the heart, but a Heart Awakening session is a gift from Spirit to help you release the illusions that have kept you from fully experiencing life. As the defense layers around the heart are peeled off, literally anything and everything can change. This is the state of grace in which miracles occur, when things happen serendipitously, where events that defy logic come together.

This is what Heart Awakening is for - to remember what is important, to remember what is real, to remember what makes a difference. It is a wake-up call from the soul saying, "Remember the journey you have embarked upon. Remember your purpose. Remember your deepest inner vows to yourself to be all you can be. You don't have to settle for anything less."

Over the years, I have done many Heart Awakening sessions. Each time I share the state of deep indwelling Divine Love with someone, I feel the incredible freedom and joy of their liberated soul and its longing to make up for all the time spent following the dictates of the outer mind. When the latent desires of the soul are released into waking consciousness, our intention to become all we can be is restored. For many of us, Heart Awakening is the key that takes us from not knowing, not caring, not being able, into tasting enough of the Divine nectar within ourselves to feel a thrust of energy and the motivation to live life to the fullest again. A taste of Love within is a reminder of the God force within, a reminder of the inner presence that makes life worth living.

To a humanity filled with peace and love - Raoult

Heart Awakening
Your Path to Unconditional Love & Healing

PART A
CREATING HEART AWAKENING

CHAPTER 1

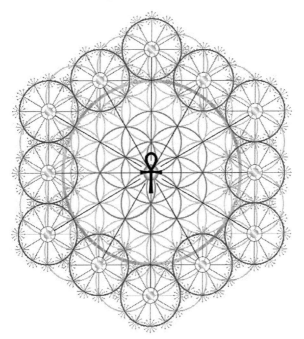

SEARCHING FOR LIFE'S PURPOSE

N o matter how challenging or difficult Earth may seem, rebirth into the true, lasting joy and beauty of life is possible. The force of Divine Love is so omniscient and so omnipotent that no matter how far away it can appear at times, the return to its path is inevitable. I discovered this truth from my own life experiences, and am grateful I am still here to tell the story.

At an early age I could remember a feeling of space and beauty from the time before I was born. I avoided anything that threatened this precious memory and hung on to it as the years passed. Remembering the grandeur, and the all-encompassing love and beauty of the spiritual world, was my Source, my inspiration, and the thread from which I knew I had to expand in this life. As I grew older, my memory of the Spirit world became dimmer, but I knew some day I would have the opportunity to bring it back to full consciousness.

During my childhood, I wanted to share my vivid spiritual memories, but I could not find any circumstance or situation where it was appropriate. I searched in vain for paths that would allow me to expand and express the energy of my true Self.

The result was a gradual rebellion against conventional life choices that appeared to take away my freedom. I realized it was more important for me to hold on to the integrity of my identity than to adapt to a world that would ignore the true potential of what life could be: joyful, pulsating, vibrant, alive, free and ecstatic. I recognized that this knowing was so precious that I promised myself always to remember it.

I wanted desperately to share this with others, but doing so within the context of everyday life seemed impossible. I gradually learned to fit in and conform, but I never felt that I really "belonged" and I could never forget the memory of my own true Self.

The Material World

Born to an English mother and a French father during their stay in Seattle, Washington, I was taken back and forth between England and France for most of my childhood. It was a tumultuous beginning, but at least I enjoyed a deep feeling of genuine love from my mother and father during my early childhood years.

One day during summer vacation, when I was about seven, my mother and father took me to the south of France, presumably for a short visit with my grandparents. But to my surprise, after we arrived, Mother told me that she and my father were leaving to create a new life in Canada, and that my younger brother and I would follow as soon as they were settled. I could hardly believe that I wasn't going with them straight away, but that wasn't the worst of it. I felt I would never see them again, and in fact it was over a year before I did.

Even though in many ways my time in the countryside in the south of France was wonderful, at times I could not help but feel upset that my parents, whom I loved and trusted so much, had left me behind, and I had no idea why. From then on, the natural expression of the free, joyful self I had remembered from birth was not the same. Later, I was to see that remembering a place of bliss did not by itself equip me to deal with life on Earth with sustained love.

Another major incident occurred when I was ten years old and living in England. My grandfather was driving me from my mother's house to his own when an oncoming car hit us at sixty miles an hour. The next thing I knew I was lying in a pool of blood on the floor of a near-by paint shop. I was unable to breathe, fading in and out. For the first time I felt fear - real fear. Then I lost consciousness.

I awoke in a hospital. My teeth had been knocked out. My right lung had collapsed and a plastic tube inserted into my chest was providing me with oxygen. I felt life had dealt me another blow. After the accident I didn't know how to regain my physical strength. I felt frail and angry at my life situation.

Sex, Drugs, Rock and Roll

While at school, I discovered other interests, many of which relied on my ability to communicate: music, entrepreneurship - selling old juke-box records at school, dealing in old comics - and I developed the ability to absorb everything about topics that interested me, such as spending all one summer making sacred geometric models.

I was very active in sports - rackets, cricket, trampolining – despite a constant pain in my lower right lung. Each time I breathed too deeply, the pain worsened. If I hiccuped, I doubled up in pain. My solution was to breathe less and less and to feel less and less. Sometimes when I was standing, a sharp pain would burst through the bottom of my lung. I would gasp and find myself flat on the floor recovering from a temporary blackout. Doctors could find nothing, do nothing and generally didn't seem to care. Or at least that was the way I perceived it.

Inevitably, my sense of rebelliousness deepened, followed by drug use, which seemed to offer a way out of the everyday world and a possibility of recapturing the joy I was born with.

Although I didn't realize it at the time, my intuition was guiding me through many experiences, so that I acquired a deep understanding of how the growth of the inner world can be frustrated by the obstacles and temptations – such as sex, drugs and rock and roll in the sixties – that cause an imbalance between inner and outer worlds. Throughout these years of seeking, I was always helping other people to find the right way for them.

I knew an ordinary nine-to-five job would not allow me to regain my sense of my true Self I remembered from childhood or allow its full expression, so I picked up a bass guitar, grew my hair long, and dropped out of college. This was "it." I formed a band and we had great fun. The companionship and the music reawakened the ability to enjoy myself.

However between the pot and the pain, my body

7

was wasting away. I was eighteen when my lung collapsed again during a rock concert. While lying in a hospital emergency room, I contemplated my life and where it was taking me. It couldn't continue in the same way. In order to heal myself I felt I should travel abroad. First, I imported cars from Germany to make money. Then I spent the best part of a year doing currency deals in Greece where many friends came to visit. The excitement of travel helped my mind and body to heal quickly, and opened up endless opportunities for further travel and for making money.

One day I felt what I really wanted to do was play with lions in their natural habitat. I took a plane to South Africa and was introduced to a couple in Capetown who generously extended their hospitality.

Shortly afterwards, a new romance began to blossom. I met Linda, a lively, talented air-brush artist with a passion for travel and adventure. My desire to explore the heart of southern Africa and its wild life inspired us to meet nature head-on in its rawest and most exhilarating state. High on love and the bliss of ignorance, we drove off through the Kalahari Desert of Botswana to meet the lions.

A professional explorer told me this journey had been done only once before. It didn't matter; my heart needed fulfillment. Totally unequipped, Linda and I ended up pushing our VW across the treacherous desert until we reached "Crocodile Camp" located at the edge of the Okavango Swamp, the largest swamp in the world. The swamp sits in the middle of the Moremi Game Reserve, which contains one of the largest concentrations of African wildlife in its natural habitat. Strangely enough, the lions we wanted to see lived on a floating island in the middle of the swamp called "Chief's Island."

After finding a local guide, we rented a dugout canoe and paddled off to Chief's Island, a four-day journey. During the day we were bombarded by tsetse flies and at night we slept on a variety of floating islands, hardly able to see the full moon on a clear night because of the millions of mosquitoes. We were bitten from head to toe.

Eventually we arrived at Chief's Island. The lions were there. So were the boa constrictors and the fourteen-foot anthills – so common we never even took a picture of them.

Looking a lion in the face filled me with awe. It didn't matter what I had gone through up to this point. Somehow this experience allowed me to recapture a part of myself I had lost hope of ever finding again. It was my first taste of releasing the anger and remembering the feeling of power, joy and unlimited potential I knew was in me as a child. The dangers of meeting a lion in the wild didn't enter my mind. It was so exhilarating all fear vanished. For the first time in a long, long time I felt free of the entrapments of the everyday natural world.

Our boat trip back to Moremi after seeing the lions was even more challenging. We ran completely out of food, and (wouldn't you know it), it rained continually during the trip – for the first time during that season of the year in twenty-six years.

The Entrepreneurial Life

In July, 1976 I bought a one-way ticket from England to New York City. Determined to make the most of the "land of opportunity," I took what money I had and bought another VW camper. I rebuilt it and set off for California, but somewhere in Georgia I took a wrong turn and ended up in Florida. I arrived in Fort Lauderdale with my money running low and nowhere to go. Desperate, I used a telephone booth as my phone number to apply for jobs, sleeping in my van near the booth at night.

Finally, I secured a job as a waiter, invested my last thirty dollars for the required coat and tie, and went to work. I was fired after two hours.

I tried various ways of making money, including selling old comics, ComputaCar (helping people to find their ideal car), and real estate – eventually owning and managing a portfolio of about four hundred rental units. This also involved listening to people's problems and developing compassion and patience for all kinds of people in all types of situations.

Living in Florida fulfilled part of my dream because at last I could enjoy all year round the weather, the beach, warm ocean, palm trees, a sense of openness and many things to explore. My teenage vision of becoming a millionaire had been fulfilled, and I had filled four passports travelling around the world, but I had not found inner joy or developed my gift for healing.

As was my modus operandi by now, I left my problems and brief marriage in Miami and moved to Winter Park, Florida, to make use of my knowledge and experience in real estate.

After almost two years of full time study a business broker called and asked, "Are you interested in buying a roof truss manufacturing plant in Ocala, Florida?" I had two questions. One was, "Where is Ocala?" and the second was, "What are roof trusses?" Within forty-eight hours I had placed a contract with a ninety-day closing to buy the plant for $650,000 – cash I didn't have. All I had were faith and guts. It was the fastest ninety days I ever experienced, and the money to complete the purchase came through only on the very last day. After a year I appointed a general manager and the company was a success, doubling its sales.

But I was physically exhausted. On my return from a trip to Egypt, I realized there might be a relationship between the pyramids and the pyramid shaped roof trusses I was manufacturing. It reawakened my interest in sacred geometry and this in turn stimulated my spiritual development in harmony with my material world.

CHAPTER 2

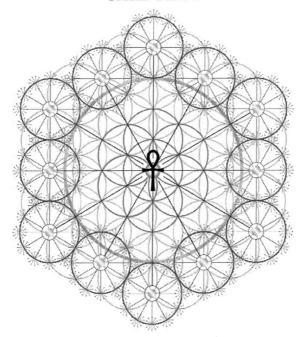

WAKING UP

During my years as an entrepreneur, I was an avid consumer of the alternative healing arts, but nothing I tried came close to the depth of healing I needed for myself. Each modality had something to offer, yet I was always left feeling there had to be a more rewarding, more effective and less tedious way to heal myself and others on every level.

My Spiritual Search

I explored many popular healing modalities, and observed the gifts and limitations of each. I studied shamanic healing with a Native American Indian teacher, and then assimilated as much Buddhist, Christian, esoteric and metaphysical knowledge as I could handle.

Out of the desire to improve the quality of my life I began doing private healing sessions based on intuitive counseling, breath work, and energy balancing. I was grateful for all I had learned from the other modalities, yet knew that my own true work involved strengthening my intuitive connection. What I was looking to create was a healing modality that would - in the simplest and most efficient way - allow the indwelling divine presence of each person to manifest.

In 1986, while still living in Florida, I met a spiritual healer by the name of Ron Hall who did a type of spiritual healing that seemed particularly appealing to me. I felt I had at last found a teaching that could help me to reconnect with my true spiritual self. Ron understood the nature of Divine Love within and the need to experience that love as an essential part of our everyday lives. My work with him became a major catalyst of my own experience and understanding of spiritual awakening. He taught of the need to release the grip that our minds have on reality. This is the key that allows us to live in our hearts – the center of Divine energy and love that makes living a joy rather than a struggle.

In 1987, I attended a retreat led by Ron outside Guadalajara in Mexico. I was soaking in a hot springs with a group of friends when I felt suddenly compelled to look up. I was astounded to see a being in scintillating, bluish light standing before me. With a soft, gentle voice he said, "Follow your heart." At the same time he telepathically told me, "You have searched everywhere in life for everything you can find, except the truth of what is in your own heart. Follow it, listen to it, and everything you want in the way of accomplishments or happiness will follow. It is your heritage; it is your birthright to know this Love. Live by it, and it will serve you more than you can possibly imagine. For all that is born of it is truth, and all that is not is illusion." Then, in a flash, he was gone.

On the morning of the last day of the retreat, one man lay on the table to await healing. Another man and I were seized by a force that moved us to the table. As we stood there, a beam of pure and incredibly intense white light suddenly appeared from above and split into two streams directly above our heads pouring into our crown chakras. The energy was so intense that the other man fainted. Terrified, I remained on my feet, not knowing what to do. A part of me wanted to turn and run as fast as I was able from a situation that now seemed to have gone far beyond the rational "controllable" world I had created for myself.

But in spite of the terror, I could not resist this guiding force. I automatically began passing my hands through the man's aura as he lay there quietly on the table. Shaking with fear, I heard my own inner voice telling me that this energy was serious, that it was bringing an opportunity for immense transformation – if I could accept it. Pushing down my fear and panic, I let myself sink more and more deeply into the energy. My whole body began trembling as the force of the energy began to pulse throughout my body. I saw in an instant the futility of the life I was living – an endless pursuit of meaningless accomplishments. The fullness of the revelation broke upon consciousness, and I reached down into the depths of my soul as far as I could feel. Suddenly I felt myself forming a determination that was deeper and more resolved than anything I had every done in my life. I now knew that I would never be content to live as I had in the past. With the purest and most sincere intention that I have ever formed in my life, I found myself saying, "*No matter what may have happened in the past or will happen in the future, I now commit fully and wholly to a life based on*

love instead of fear – no matter what the consequences." In
that moment I completely and irrevocably committed
my life to the path of unconditional love – and Heart
Awakening was born.

At that instant, an intense vibration began pulsing
at the base of my spinal column. Suddenly, a massive
jolt of energy shot up my spine and throughout my
body, literally lifting me eighteen inches into the air.
It was an incredible experience. My heart poured
open. Tears streamed down my face. The only thing
I was conscious of was Divine Love. The vastness of
it was almost too much for my body to handle.
Within the love I discovered a place so sacred and
pure it fulfilled all the longings I ever had or could
possibly ever have. It was right there, in my heart,
simply forgotten and buried underneath the hubbub
of my egocentric dramas. I had been willing to
relearn all, to give up all. In return, I was given
everything. It was a place so pure I felt I could and
would never leave it. I realized everything in my life
up to that point had been based on illusion, yet I saw
it had all been necessary to prepare me for a direct
experience of Divine bliss and Divine Love.

I now had all the strength I needed. I realized I
had never been disconnected from Divine Love – to
grow in it was to share in it. My work was to help
others find this Love inside themselves and peel off
the illusion of what was not, and to reveal what had
always been. I was astounded at how deeply I could
go into this Love and how far I had separated myself
from it. It was like coming out of a dream. My

childhood memory of my true Self was back in full force. At last I remembered who I was and what I was. This reawakening was God's gift to me, part of my soul's destiny. When my ego was ready to let go, my soul's purpose could begin to be fulfilled.

And what I realized from my experience was that this is the true purpose of healing: to open the heart and set the soul free, to live in a deep knowing of the inherent Divine perfection within all things and all people. True healing means releasing the ways of the ego, trusting in the Divine plan, and living moment to moment to fulfill the soul's desire to see and live life from a divine perspective.

At last I was receiving answers to the questions I had been asking for so long. True healing heals our relationship with our Divine Self, and Love is the doorway through which we all must pass. Everything I had learned intellectually now made practical sense. On the journey into Divine Love, pain is dissolved and truth revealed.

After the retreat I returned to Florida, embracing my commitment to demonstrate how Divine Love heals all. Having found that place inside me, I felt that I could help others find it within themselves. I thought of the many healers I knew who were searching for this inner Love, and wondered how I could share what I had experienced with them. What would happen to their work if they experienced it — and what if they in turn could help others experience it too?

As Heart Awakening evolved, it didn't seem to fit

into any traditional category of healing. Rather, many people experienced it as a bridge between conventional therapies and a true spiritual awakening. For myself and those I worked with in applying this "heart awakening" energy, it seemed as though we had been given a new direction revealed by Spirit. Its purpose is to release the negativity in the emotional body and open the heart to experience the actual feeling of God's Love for ourselves and others. I felt I had experienced a state of consciousness normally only experienced in the Spirit realm. It was a state in which all things could be healed because of the clarity and certainty of soul level perception.

I realized that Heart Awakening is a way of healing that guides and assists each person to experience for themselves God's love and wisdom. In this freedom the soul's energy, purpose and direction are gradually revealed, and the soul, with the cooperation of the personality, embarks on a meaningful plan for its life. Its activity takes on a new momentum and direction.

My Personal Healing

The healing retreat in Mexico opened my heart in more ways than one. In the same week that Heart Awakening was revealed to me, I met Wauneta. Although a year passed before we moved in together, when we first met it was as though we had always known each other. The full opening of my heart had immediately brought me the love relationship I had always sought, full of synergy and natural compatibility. Wauneta and I traded healing sessions, which helped Heart Awakening develop. My understanding of its essence was complete, but I needed to learn how to help others experience it. Because of the sessions with Wauneta, the healings I received from Ron, and what I was learning in my own spiritual practice, my life began coming back into proper balance. All of these sessions helped me grow by learning to surrender the ways of the ego, come back into the heart, see things through the heart, and build a new life around the ways of Spirit.

My fears about the financial effects of leaving the business world for a spiritual healing life were unfounded. More and more people wanted sessions, and I sold the profitable roof truss company a year later.

Each Heart Awakening session deepened my perception of Divine Love. I was continually learning about the depth of wisdom that it contains: that the universe is abundant, that things are taken care of, and that I could rely on the magnetic quality of the Divine Love within.

When I was in my heart, manifestation became so much easier and I seemed to need less. I felt more content with the pleasures of living in a heart-awakened state, and a wealth of new friends and acquaintances entered my life. For the first time, I was aware of how simple life can be when we follow its natural flow.

During my healing sessions, I reviewed my life,

learning to accept my own Divine Child, to love myself and the people I knew. I went back into the traumas of my past and saw them the way Spirit had intended for me to see them. Each Heart Awakening session dissolved more and more of the pain I had been running away from. Gradually, I felt safe enough to go within myself and heal much of how I had felt about damaging my body when I was young. Each time I was willing to see how the Divine perfection and the Divine Love had always been available to me, I realized just how much of my life had existed in a vacuum of illusion. By forgetting the ever-present nature of the Divine Love within, I had imagined it to be unreachable and separate from my everyday existence. In reality the Love had never gone away.

My body started to heal. The growing pains of my youth gradually melted away. I even realized that the unhappy experiences with my parents were really great gifts in disguise. What I found was an ability to see any situation from a higher perspective so that it could be used in line with the Divine plan.

Whenever I lost the awareness of Divine Love and perfection, giving or receiving a Heart Awakening session released whatever issues were in the way, and I was able to recapture and maintain the happiness of living in harmony with the soul's true purpose and life plan. Tasting what was possible gave me the courage and desire to go on until a full Heart Awakened state was reached. Some sessions even took me back into past life experiences. Those memories and situations explained much of what was going on in the present that I couldn't have understood otherwise. But although things were going so well, I still had many lessons to learn, some very difficult.

Among them were: learning to keep myself as a practitioner in balance on every level - physical, emotional, mental and spiritual; understanding and removing discarnate entities; learning to see chakras and the aura; clearing energy fields so that each client could live the life he or she came to live; opening their energy channels to facilitate soul connection, and teaching how to deepen levels of awareness so that they could become a divine loving presence on earth.

The problems that clients arrive with often have very deep unconscious roots; so the work done during a Heart Awakening session is profound and cannot always be explained in words for some time afterwards, but the effect can always be felt. The work has manifested superbly in the lives of many former clients who became students of Heart Awakening and who have gone on with open hearts to develop their own line of work successfully.

I had a further challenge to face in my own life. Wauneta and I had been deeply in love, living together in California and Arizona and trading sessions for several happy years until she died, leaving me feeling quite bereft.

The Meaning of Heart Awakening

With Wauneta gone, I began doing Heart
Awakening sessions more intensely, and I received a
valuable gift, one of the keys to my own healing and
the healing of others: I began to see the aura clairvoy-
antly.

At first I had to go through an intense learning
curve regarding how to manage energy fields. I started to see the energetic effects of the staggering
panorama of psychological patterns within the aura,
and how they inhibited a person from realizing the
full potential of their soul's journey. I saw how emotions caused leaks, tears and other damage to the layers of the aura and the chakras. I witnessed how the
qualities of purity, love and joy infuse the aura with a
kaleidoscope of beautiful colors and how the etheric
substance that they magnetized was so important in a
person's ability to express their true spirit personality.
I began to understand how much easier it is to heal
deep emotional wounds when corresponding repair
work is done to the electromagnetic field that surrounds the body. Surprisingly, I started to see that it
was not just the negative emotion that blocked the
subtle bodies; intensely strong positive desires of the
ego personality for success in career, relationships,
money and health, if misguided, created major energetic distortions of their own.

I learned to meditate on the Divine presence within until the wisdom could be shared with the client.
Deep levels of consciousness in high states of medita-

tion brought a Divine perspective on any situation that a person was experiencing.

I learned to recognize thought forms in people's auras, and to restore their spiritual insight, creating an energetic balance as a way of living for the Self. A clean, clear aura enables people to manifest the very best in their lives; the clearer the aura, the more effectively God's energy can flow into their activities.

To learn more about the science of energy healing, I began a deep study of the oriental art of QiGong (Chi-Gong). Qi means life-force energy and Gong means practice – in other words the art of cultivating the flow of life-force energy through our body no matter where we are or what we are doing. We continually utilize our life-force energy; therefore mastering the art of using it became an important stepping stone in my on-going development of the Heart Awakening work.

I now knew beyond a shadow of doubt that God sees all of us only in perfection, and the universe is always functioning in perfection. He knows that each of us will some day come to realize these truths and that this realization will give us the power to fully express the vastness of Divine Love that resides in the depths of our hearts.

As the years passed, the Heart Awakening work became even more powerful. Each day I asked for the deepening of my gifts and understanding of the Divine, and each day I was taught how to draw the energy into the healing and where to focus my attention. Miracles occurred to the extent that I could handle them and gradually my commitment to live a Heart Awakened life became a reality.

After more than twenty years I have found that the greatest gift I can give myself is to help others reach deeply within themselves and honestly say, "This is it. This is the place, the feeling of my true spiritual Self – I am now experiencing the very essence of my divine life." They can then see the divinity in others and in the whole manifest world, and articulate it. This keeps the doors of communication between ourselves and others permanently open in the etheric field and the soul works to keep it open in the everyday world.

I find great joy in seeing the enormous shifts in consciousness that have occurred for thousands of people who were longing to free themselves from struggle and suffering, and who can now feel the freedom, peace and happiness that comes from the direct experience of unconditional love.

For most people the Heart Awakening experience is life transforming. It opens up a profound understanding of life and shows the right direction to take for spiritual growth.

Many people believe, consciously or unconsciously, that the only way to experience the fullness of divine life is to leave their body through physical death. In reality, the very opposite is true. You can live that life right here and now. All it requires is a willingness to change your perceptions and open your heart.

This was God's gift to me and it is now my gift to you.

PART B
WHAT IS HEART AWAKENING?

CHAPTER 3

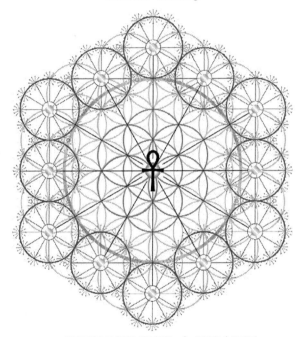

UNFOLDING A HEART
AWAKENING SESSION

What is it like to receive a Heart Awakening session? Every person's experience is different, and every Heart Awakener is different. Yet the blend of giver and receiver is somehow perfect each and every time. If you decide to have a session, Spirit leads you to the Heart Awakener who has the perceptions and life experiences most needed to help you.

I have found that each person who gives a Heart Awakening to another also receives insight into what they need for their own healing. So no matter what situation you are in, the light of Spirit will carry its message - both for the person receiving the session and the person giving it. Confidentiality is always respected and observed by Heart Awakeners, but what transpires in a session is more in the realm of Divine revelation, bringing with it such deep insight and profound change over time, that many feel inspired to share what happens with others.

We all have unconscious thoughts and emotions that undermine our personal and spiritual growth, and prevent us from accepting and loving ourselves. A Heart Awakening session need not be painful or dramatic or over-long. It allows you to receive from your Self what is truly yours. Sprit moves through you, encouraging you to communicate what your heart needs to be free. What you can express, you can heal.

Sessions often bring up memories needing reconciliation; indeed most of us have things we are afraid to look at. But the Heart Awakening energy, coupled with the healing power of your inner Self, creates a journey of discovery and release rather than something to be feared.

Behind every trapped, suppressed memory is a gift from Spirit, and that awareness far outweighs the benefits of holding on to the past. The purpose of Heart Awakening sessions is to help you awaken to that gift. Because of the purity of the intention that is set within the session, when you call on the unconscious memories to surface, you will always be shown what you need to remember and resolve.

The process is as natural as can be. You are simply invited into an unconditionally loving and safe environment where you can be as free and open as you like. All you need is the willingness to let go and express what you see and feel during the session. Heart awakeners are so in tune with divine energy that they are not judging your processing or words. They are simply seeking to help you align with that energy.

This is one of the distinct differences between Heart Awakening and conventional counseling and coaching. The personality self of both Heart Awakener and client are set aside as the inner Self begins to reveal itself. This is of utmost importance because this is the part of ourselves that can actually make any change that our heart and souls need to make. Many times, after a first session, clients have told me that they were shocked to hear what was coming out of their mouths, and as a result they shut down, fearful of saying the 'wrong thing' - things that might be disloyal or offensive to themselves, to loved ones or to life in general. But in reality, what-

ever comes out of your mouth, or whatever constructive emotions are revealed during a session, are exactly those things that most need to be expressed. And
everything you do express in these moments forms a
precious and profoundly private, intimate and unconditionally loving dialog between you and your own
Higher Self.

So, when you come for a Heart Awakening, be prepared for the unexpected. Our egos have been socially
conditioned over so many years that they will almost
always rebel against what the heart and soul most
want to express. Before you come for a session, reas-
sure your outer self, your ego, that you want only the
best for yourself, and that you are seeking to restore
the fullness of the Divine Love and awareness that is
the spiritual reality behind our outer minds.

Solving Any Problem

The healing process in Heart Awakening is based
on the understanding that, in spite of the problems
you may have created for yourself, Spirit has already
provided the solution. Sessions naturally allow you to
be freed from the illusions of your outer mind, your
ego and your personality and to be reconnected to
your inner Self. It is this reconnection that will allow
you to know exactly what to do in life - which career
to follow, which relationships are constructive and fulfilling, where to live, what to buy, how to relate to
your mother, your husband, your children. Sound too
good to be true? The fact is that your inner Self is
your Divine Self, and your truest connection to God.
There is absolutely nothing in your life that is a mys-

tery or a problem to your inner Self. The problem of being human has always been that we just don't seem to know how to get in touch with and stay connected to this divine aspect of ourselves that contains all of the wisdom and guidance we will ever need to fulfill our learning and evolution on earth. But as I discovered through personal experience, the Heart Awakening energy will guide you to this reconnection when you are truly ready to begin.

The Three Parts of Heart Awakening

There are three primary parts to the Heart Awakening session. The first is an intuitive spiritual counseling, followed by energy work in the aura, which leads to the unique spiritual transformation called the Heart Awakening Breakthrough.

1. Intuitive Spiritual Counseling

The first part of the Heart Awakening session is devoted to a period of spiritual intuitive counseling. This counseling can last from a few minutes to an hour or more, depending on your current needs. You are given the opportunity to express what is happening in your life and what you would like to focus on during the session. If you don't know exactly what your issues are, that's fine. The initial counseling period generally opens up a discussion between the two of you about points of most concern to you. Many times the Heart Awakener will intuitively receive an insight which brings forth an important and often surprising message relevant to your particular situation. The counseling process is generally deeply intuitive, yet loving and reassuring, so feel free to ask whatever questions you might have.

2. Energy Work

Once the intuitive spiritual counseling period is finished, the Heart Awakener invites you to lie on a therapeutic massage table in a relaxed and comfortable position. Now the energy work on the aura begins.

Soothing music follows an opening prayer which is guided by Spirit.

The specific desire and request for your healing is expressed aloud by the Heart Awakener in a gentle and loving tone. The Awakener then steps gently into the electromagnetic energy field surrounding your body and the work begins.

Energy work is done on a soul level guided by Spirit. There is no set pattern or formula - simply a flow that unfolds to help you experience a deep, open space within the heart. The purpose of the energy work is to clear the aura of distortions and restore it to proper balance and harmony.

The principles of the Heart Awakening energy work can be understood from even basic levels of science. All material things are formed from atomic particles which are in a state of constant motion. This perpetual motion of electrons, protons and other atomic particles generates the force we call energy. Everything which exists in the material world is 'energized,' even those things which appear to be inanimate such as rocks, minerals, etc.

Conglomerates of moving atomic particles form

energy 'fields' of varying sizes which move and vibrate at different levels of frequency (or rates of speed). To most of us, these energy fields are invisible, but if we could see them, they would probably appear as vibrating, pulsating strata, moving at varying rates of speed, much like clouds, covering everything. Vibrating energy fields are also affected by the magnetic forces of the earth, and in this context are referred to as 'electro-magnetic fields' created by the earth's rotation around its iron core. This movement of atoms and their electrically-charged particles is a continuous invisible presence that surrounds us, affecting us and our lives continuously and in every way imaginable, whether or not we are aware of it.

Today, science has made some of these all-pervasive invisible energy fields visible through media that use them, such as radios, TVs, telephones, etc. But, in general, scientists have been much less interested in determining other roles that energy fields or electro-magnetic energies play in what still remain invisible arenas of our lives. We cannot see the energy fields that surround our bodies, yet we now know that they are there. The same invisible atomic particles that make up rocks, trees and everything else that exists, form the basis of our bodies too. We are surrounded by these energy fields, yet we know little or nothing about them.

Historically, the study of the effects of invisible energies on our everyday lives has been the domain of human endeavors such as religion, spirituality, philosophy, astrology, and metaphysics. Modern scientists sometimes scorn some of these types of observation of the material world because they feel that the conclusions drawn from them are formed and 'clouded' by human emotions that are fickle and unreliable.

But what scientists have failed to take into account is that human beings were aware of invisible energies long before modern science discovered the atom. Even what we call the 'lower animals' hear and see things that we do not. Invisible energies and electromagnetic fields are all around us, and we need to acknowledge this reality and its effect on us if we are to have any lasting happiness, serenity or order in our lives.

The invisible energy fields around our bodies contain moving, pulsating, vibrating atomic particles which move at a certain speed or 'frequency' (also referred to as a 'vibration'). These energy fields have been sensed by humans throughout the course of history (the 'halos' around pictures of Holy men and women), and today are referred to as auras. Again, current science seems to detest this word, and yet someone had to call these energy fields something.

The important thing for us to realize is that the faster the atomic particles around us vibrate, the less dense the particles become and the more energy they release. We can see this principle at work in atomic power plants in which the movement of atomic particles in the reactor is increased enormously by exposure to radioactive elements such as plutonium. The faster the atoms move, the more energy is released, which is then converted into electricity and heat to run the innumerable technological marvels that make up our modern civilization.

What does this mean for our own individual power plants - our bodies? It means that if we speed up the atomic particles within our own energy fields we'll feel better, get sick less often (if at all), feel happier, know more, have richer, fuller, more meaningful lives and so on and so on. Why? Because higher frequencies or vibrations (faster moving atomic particles in our energy fields) equals more and more energy which equals more power which generates an explosion of potential new realities (just like the atomic power plants).

Increasing the frequency (or rate of speed) of atomic structures also increases the rate of energy release, and for human beings, increase in energy lends a sense of happiness, euphoria, and a heightened sense of well-being and power. So how do we get the atomic particles generated by our bodies to move faster so that we can experience more energy and a heightened sense of awareness? We remove the influences that slow the movement of our bodies' atomic particles and sap energy, such as extreme amounts of dense foods (meats, junk foods), synthetic substances, cigarettes, violence, and so on.

Energy fields of different frequencies do affect each other, as we see when radioactive elements are put in contact with and destroy substances vibrating at different rates of speed. The more we allow ourselves to be exposed to substances whose vibratory rates deteriorate our own, the worse we feel, physically, emotionally and mentally. It's critical to your health, well-being and continued evolution that you determine which foods, medicines, environments, etc. have the vibratory level that suit you best. Each person's atomic structure is different, and likewise each individual's frequency level and needs.

Another important step in keeping your vibratory levels high is to clear away energies of destructive vibration that have become imbedded in your individual energy fields. Years of childhood trauma, abuse, violence, emotions of depression, despair, anger and hatred significantly alter and distort the free-flowing movements of people's energy fields, especially because these intense emotions carry highly-charged frequencies which are unlike the natural state at which our bodies operate best. Once these energies enter our auras or electro-magnetic fields, they are difficult to remove, and begin to interfere with all the energy systems of the body. This results in metabolic disturbances which give rise to digestive problems, chronic fatigue, organ malfunction, abnormal cell growth, psychological disturbances, etc. which even decades of drugs, counseling and other therapies cannot remove.

In a way, electromagnetic or energy fields look to me much like blood cells seen under a microscope. Healthy blood cells are well spaced out and move freely and vigorously within the lymph fluid. They give me the impression of looking 'bouncy', and full of life. On the other hand, unhealthy blood cells are often clumped together, and appear sluggish, deformed and drained of life and vitality. Energy fields display these same characteristics. The atoms and atomic particles in the energy fields of well-balanced, healthy individuals move freely with vitality and energy, while those in energy fields fraught with damage and trauma appear distorted and drained of vitality. Many times I have been aware of a person's nearness to death, even before they tell me that they have a terminal disease, simply by looking at the feeble and disordered movement of the atoms within their electromagnetic fields.

This is why the energy work of the Heart Awakening session is so important. During the session, I can actually see or sense the damage that has been done to a person's energy or electromagnetic field, and I am given the guidance to see how and where to remove the damaging energies of past trauma, chronic psychological stress and life experiences. Once these damaging energies are removed and released, I can see that the normal function of the atoms in the person's energy field is restored.

Experiencing the Power of Thought

People often do not realize the power that thoughts, emotions and feelings have on their energy fields, or auras. Beliefs, thoughts and feelings are forms that actually generate their own energy fields. When the energy fields of thought forms are injected into your energy field, they create distortions and being magnetic in nature, attract and accumulate similar thought forms. Ultimately a fixed pattern is formed that becomes very hard to release, and we continue to re-attract people and situations into our lives we know are not for our highest good, over and over again.

During the Heart Awakening, the energies of these

imbedded, limiting thought forms are visible to me as dark areas of different size and intensity within the aura, varying from deep black to shades of gray. Deep, chronic, intense pain, grief or despair produce the darker colors, while thought-forms of lesser intensity may appear as gray or murky yellow. In one instance, a woman came to me for a Heart Awakening and I was taken aback when I saw that almost the entire energy field surrounding her body was a profoundly deep shade of black. I asked her if she had been contemplating suicide and she told me that she had actually made a recent suicide attempt, as a result of unresolved emotional disturbances stemming from severe abuse suffered in childhood, for which she had received extensive therapy without success.

We worked together for many weeks, and as I cleared and removed the damaged energies from her electromagnetic field, her psychological state significantly improved, along with her physical health and sense of well-being. Eventually, she returned to work and is living a happy, well-balanced, fulfilling life.

Layers of chronic, congested negative thought patterns within the energy field are generally very thick, so even though you may experience the full impact of a Heart Awakening in a single session, it might take several sessions over a period of time to help unlock the deepest psychological patterns. But once the electromagnetic field is cleared and re-balanced, you can once again see, experience and know the fullness and joy of the divine energies all around us.

Experiencing the Energy Work

During the period of energy clearing, you may find yourself going deeper and deeper into a state of relaxation and might even take a short nap. All the while you may feel a build-up of energies all around you. You aren't sure what is going on, but somehow you feel your entire being is undergoing transformation and is enveloped in something extremely comfortable and pure. You feel weightless, even though your actual physical body gradually feels heavier and more relaxed. Memories surface and pass across the screen of your mind and there are often surprises - things you haven't remembered for a long time.

As the session progresses, you feel as though you are going on a journey. You may not be sure of where you are going, but a sense of adventure restores your certainty. You know something is different, something has changed, though you aren't sure what. Somehow your normal mechanisms of responding to thoughts and feelings seem different. You drift into a sense of timelessness and an extraordinarily heightened state of awareness - even deeper than meditation. You have no idea whether a few minutes have passed or a few hours and you really don't care because the present moment seems to encompass everything of value. You may become aware of guides and teachers on the inner planes communicating with you or simply making their presence felt.

Gradually, you notice significant changes on levels you never conceived possible. The purpose may seem unclear at first, even though a part of you feels you do know and should remember. You begin to shift and change in ways somehow familiar yet hard to articulate. Meanwhile, you may become aware of parts of your energy field in need of attention and of deeply buried issues starting to surface.

3. The Breakthrough

After a while, the Heart Awakener gently begins speaking to you, guiding you through layers of your subconscious on a journey into the center of your heart. During this third stage, you recognize that you are in a heightened state of consciousness. When the Heart Awakener speaks to you, responding may be difficult at first, but as you begin to talk the energy surrounding you supports you in knowing what to say, bringing to the surface of your consciousness memories you had forgotten. As these are expressed, you find yourself able to absorb the Divine energy more deeply.

Each time you communicate your true feelings, the energy moves in, until Spirit makes its purpose known and Divine perfection reveals itself. Tears may flow, releasing toxins from your emotional body. Negative emotions are released as the energy moves deeper and deeper through you and you express what has separated you from the Divine Love for so long.

As this natural unraveling occurs, you are never pushed in any direction. You are invited into those places where you know you most want and need to go and when you allow the natural expression of what you are experiencing, Spirit moves in. Gradually, you recognize how much of yourself has been separated from the Divine Love and begin to see and feel everything in its relationship to that Love. The more willing you are to forgive and allow Spirit within you to come alive, the more the old patterns melt away.

Your part in the Heart Awakening is to articulate any physical, mental or emotional joy or pain you feel. Any psychological situation starts in the outer layers of the aura and gradually works its way inward, finally manifesting as a physical problem. During the session, you recognize how deeply you can go into some of these areas. Previously unreachable areas suddenly become very clear and the raising of energy makes it impossible to hold onto these issues. You realize that behind each pattern of pain, Spirit's healing power waits to reveal itself to you, and your willingness to accept Spirit's presence gives you the insights needed to verbally express your pain and convert it to unconditional love. Issues surface from your subconscious and patterns dissolve, never to return. The life-force energy formerly suppressed within is now restored to you.

The more open you are to Spirit and the deeper your need the more effective the session becomes. A session is like a door through which all healing can eventually occur. When this happens, the energy often rushes in so powerfully that you are flushed from head to toe with an infusion of Divine energy. Generally this happens in the first session. The timing depends on the stress levels within your body and your willingness to let go and recognize what is going on in your heart. One of the reasons the session is so simple and effective is that in general people do not recognize or experience how really loving they are.

Energy work often brings up unexpected issues. What emerges is always what a person most needs to clear. For example, many relive memories of their birth and release energetic blockages that occurred at that time. Some are taken back to specific traumas or accidents in their lives, giving them an opportunity to see the Divine purpose behind the events that influenced their perceptions of life. Quite often, people simply find themselves back at a time and place when a specific pattern began. We seldom realize how much there is to deal with until we fully open to the Divine Light inside ourselves.

One of the gifts of a Heart Awakening session is how the energy knows where to go. You don't have to expend effort determining your issues because they are revealed in a way that is just right for you. You are never given more than you can handle. The purpose of a Heart Awakening journey may not always be clear at first. However, Spirit reveals its purpose as the session progresses.

The healing energy always goes to where it is needed most. As the energies pour in, issues that caused the greatest blockages in the electromagnetic field are revealed. Based on the knowledge and understanding you had at the time, you created the thought patterns buried in the energy field. To heal those patterns, you must consciously let them go.

During a session, you can experience true forgiveness at the deepest level. This heart-opening experience dissolves all negative feelings and emotions. In our daily lives, we tend to forgive intellectually even when the emotional body isn't feeling forgiving. The energy work helps you say what needs to be said and gives you the energy to go further than you might think possible. As you express from the energy and allow your heart to unravel itself, Spirit brings you all the understanding and awareness needed to help you through.

Before the breakthrough portion begins, you may feel a sizable amount of energy above the chest. It rests there, waiting for you to speak your truth. As you speak, the layers of untruth covering your heart are released. Once everything blocking your heart is expressed, the energy pours in, and the full impact of a Heart Awakening is realized. You will also be guided on how to ground your new understanding into your everyday life.

An open heart is not something you can achieve intellectually. It is a gift that comes from your capacity to allow Spirit to show you the way to perceive things from the Divine perspective.

When a session is completed, the Heart Awakener seals your aura. A closing prayer invites blessings and releases you to Spirit's ongoing support for whatever may reveal itself as a result of the session. You trust any future unraveling will unfold in its natural process - a flow of new life born out of the Heart Awakening session.

CHAPTER 4

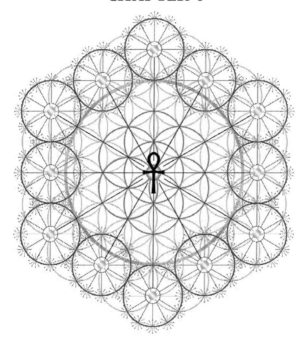

REDISCOVERING YOUR WHOLENESS

Unless you are living in a state of Divine bliss, the chances are you could use a Heart Awakening. One of the most important aspects of healing is aligning the personality with the soul so that it can develop into a soul-infused personality. The personality is the sum total of all of our thoughts and feelings. It is "what I think I am or what I feel I am" and encompasses everything we have ever created. For most of us, it is the part of ourselves that believes we are separate from God or from the universe.

The ego has long sought to have its needs fulfilled by reaching outside of itself to others, only to find disappointment and disillusionment in spite of a deep conviction it knows what it wants. The ego's attachment to outcome and form causes immense pain for the personality self. Often, it is possible to experience a reversal of this momentum within a single Heart Awakening session. This is one of the primary purposes of Heart Awakening - to help you surrender the undesirable aspects of the ego and rebuild an identity (ego/spirit) based on a solid understanding of and connection to your Divine Self.

Unwanted aspects of the ego are dissolved. Our identity as a creative expression of our connection with the Divine is rebuilt. The extent to which we can live this way depends on our capacity to release patterns of pain and suffering.

The ego begins with the word "I." Each time we think with the word "I" and begin a statement or thought with "I," it is our personality doing its dance of self-deception. Most of us identify ourselves with our personality, but this is not our true identity. A key function of a Heart Awakening session is to help you release the built-up illusions of who you think you are and reveal the truth of your soul's purpose for this life.

By simply stilling the mind in the present moment, we start to become aware of the Divine Love within and around us. To deepen our capacity to dwell in Divine Love, the unresolved and unforgiven aspects of the personality need to be dissolved. Then we are free to identify with our true Spirit and act as a Divine Self in unity with all creation. The extent to which we can live this way has a great deal to do with our capacity to release our patterns of identifying with the parts of ourselves believing themselves to be in pain and suffering.

Many of us have been stuck, often for lifetimes, recreating patterns of personality behavior so deeply ingrained they are hard to change. The accumulation of certain thought patterns creates a magnetic field in the aura that attracts more thoughts and patterns of a like nature. After a while, it is very difficult to shift these without the help of strong Divine forces.

The Heart Awakening process addresses issues that seem the most difficult to resolve. All psychological patterns that continually recreate themselves can be changed in a session if the willingness is there and the timing is right.

Sometimes people don't understand why they decided to come for a Heart Awakening session. It is a prompting from Spirit that brings you to a session, rather than anything you know or don't know about

Heart Awakening. The impulse from Spirit that guides you to ask for a session contains a prompting to be receptive. Not knowing why you came, helps to avoid preconceived ideas that might prevent you from being completely open to the adventure of the session and making the most of it. The way to approach the work is just to know it exists and, when the timing is right, you'll know you are ready for your Heart Awakening.

Others may prefer to spend some time in prayer or meditation and ask themselves what they would like out of the session. On one level, you may think you know what needs healing. However, a person's perception of the real problem often turns out to be just a surface issue, and the real issue reveals itself as the session progresses. On another level, what you think, doesn't matter, because the desire for what most needs healing is already within you. And it always surfaces. You can do no wrong. Simply being available for the highest and most beneficial healing may well be enough.

It doesn't matter if your issues revolve around relationships, a career problem, physical pain, or even a spiritual dilemma. All the problems arise from the illusion of separation from the Divine. No matter what the issue is or what direction you take, the end result is an open heart. All that is needed on your part is your willingness. No more can come up than should. You are never presented with more than you can handle. Nothing is done to make you whole or happy because the wholeness and happiness are already within you waiting to be reawakened. The purpose of the session is to help you to dissolve the layers of illusion and allow the spiritual truth, which has always been within, to be revealed at a deeper level than would otherwise be possible.

For a session to work, you must be willing to come into integrity in every area of your life, and forgive anyone for anything, especially yourself. Spirit also needs you to accept responsibility for having created your perception of the reality you are experiencing.

Separating From Your Ego

There is so much to learn on the journey to wholeness. The ego has many tricks designed to preserve itself. But you must remember that you are not your ego. The function of the Heart Awakening session is to help you step out of ego identification and into the experience of connection with Spirit. This occurs at a specific frequency and energy level. The ego resists any attempt to go toward this energy. The role of the Heart Awakener is to hold the knowingness of your perfection within the energy, to see it within you and allow you to get there by yourself. Your true self will emerge to replace the dramas of the ego that have buried your essence.

The main reason we suppress our feelings is because we don't know how to express them without withdrawing or blaming someone else. During a session, the Heart Awakener creates a safe space where you are held in Divine Love. For most of us, this is a first-time experience - to be in the unconditionally loving presence of Spirit where there is no judgment of anything we say. The feeling of safety and the presence of Spirit create the right circumstances for you to let go.

You will be amazed at what comes up and what has been suppressed. Issues you thought had been dealt with long ago can still hold their cords deep within the emotional body. Many emotional patterns move around within the energy field. During sessions, the Heart Awakener shifts these trapped emotions within the electromagnetic field, bringing them to the surface of your consciousness to be released. Spirit guides this process, with no forced technique or effect. The deeper you go into the Love, the more is revealed and the more Spirit can show its presence.

At other times, your receptivity could be so great that Spirit moves in and, within minutes, the core pattern is dissolved. Spirit knows where and what is needed, and the pattern will surface in the most appropriate way. Often it isn't your pain that needs revealing, but rather the memory of when you were a child - when you were full of your true self and knew your Divinity. Our "presence" never needs to go to the past, but the vision and the faith were also there, and you were ready for the big adventure of your life. Now the resurfacing of this memory and the energy of your true self can bring you into the fully Heart Awakened state your soul has always desired.

When you experience yourself in this way, in your perfection, nothing need be added or taken away. You become the observer of your thoughts and feelings, no longer controlled by the exterior world. You see and know yourself in your Divine nature, whole and healed. The opening to this space is a resting place. The outer mind wonders, "How am I ever going to keep this sense of wholeness and well-being?" Then suddenly you realize it has always been there and will always be there. You know you cannot ever be separated from your true Self.

The ego personality believes that there is no such thing as perfection and indeed bases its reality and its choices of action on the fundamental belief that error is real. The moment it does so, it loses its ability to know the Divine purpose behind each situation, and it experiences anger, despair, grief, rage, defeat - all because it does not realize that God, not the ego, is in control, and that all that happens, happens for a reason.

When we begin to acknowledge and accept that we are much more than our ego, and that each and every event in our lives has a meaning we can understand from the soul level, our lives change for the better. It isn't necessary to feel hurt or fearful or frustrated by life when we reconnect to the security, serenity and wisdom of our inner Selves. With this realization, the ego assumes its rightful place, and allows itself to be guided by the inner knowing of our divine minds which leads us exactly where we need to go in this life to fulfill our purpose for being here. When your outer mind stops trying to do everything, your life begins to fall into place.

Letting Go of Expectations

It is important not to have specific expectations
about a session. I once studied with an American
Indian teacher who spoke of the seven dark arrows of
the personality: Attachment; Dependency; Judgment;
Comparison; Expectation; The Lost, Needy,
Wounded, Abandoned Child; and Self-Importance.
Our personalities are fraught with fears, doubts,
demands and expectations. But in realizing this, we
can begin to separate our awareness from our personalities, realizing that the characteristics that make up
our individual personality are temporary illusions
that were born from our mistaken belief that we are
separated from God and from 'heaven' while we are
here on Earth. Life can seem impossibly complex and
difficult at times, but the first step in getting beyond
that perception is to let go of the belief that we are
our egos, that our personalities are the truth of who
we are.

By laying the personality self and its judgments
and expectations aside, you open up to the enormous
potential of what Heart Awakening has to offer you.
It is important to accept what Spirit is offering - an
unconditionally loving space to deepen the capacity
to love yourself. You don't have to believe in God or
have a particular religion to receive the full benefits
of a session. All you need is a basic willingness to
express the truth of what you are feeling. As negative emotions are released, you gradually discover a
deepening of your heart. All the spiritual wisdom
you have heard takes on a practical meaning. As you

feel the love within, you find yourself expressing its wisdom in your own unique way. Spirit is teaching you and the deeper you go, the more you accept yourself as totally divine and deserving of complete joy, freedom, fulfillment and peace.

Following a Session

Heart Awakening sessions vary from two to four or more hours in length. They take longer than most other therapies because you are invited to go deeper into yourself than you have ever gone before. Even though great benefit comes from doing sessions regularly, they cannot be done in a routine way. Each step must come from a deep desire to make a change and go to the next level.

Sessions are a means through which the next spiral of life's progress can be seeded into consciousness. Time and space need to be created for this to occur. Typically, a light schedule for a three-day period after a session is recommended. This will enable you to fully absorb all the benefits of your Heart Awakening. It isn't essential to stop working, but it is best to have a more restful schedule while you complete an old phase of life and give birth to the new. The impact is often so profound, it can take weeks or months to integrate the new knowledge into your life.

Having stable, on-going support for your spiritual awakening process will save you a tremendous amount of time and frustration. Returning for additional Heart Awakening sessions provides the support you need. Each session will reveal from within more and more of the universal truths which enable you to experience genuine spiritual living. Many people who receive Heart Awakenings already have their own spiritual or religious faiths. Yet, through Heart Awakening, these people have found they are able to experience a depth of Divine Love and truth that is more profound than anything they have ever experienced before.

When you return for regular Heart Awakening sessions, your spiritual goals will be supported. For instance, a person may return to gain the spiritual wisdom needed to improve his or her family life. Another might return to accelerate his spiritual learning or to become a healer. Heart Awakening can address any problem or issue in your life, whether it be losing weight, healing your relationships, finding your real path, or just learning to enjoy living on a deeper level.

The form of a Heart Awakening may differ from one person to another. Because it is an expression of Spirit, a session is very fluid and flexible and the present moment always prevails. In the highest sense, Heart Awakening enables you to experience the inherent Divinity within every situation. You find you can step out of the realm of conflict, despair and disillusionment into a higher frequency of Divine Love, joy and perfection. By accessing the frequency of your soul's connection with the Divine, you can draw on its wisdom so that you can fulfill your purpose on Earth.

As I say these words, I realize that simply giving you this information about Heart Awakening is one thing, while the quality of the energy is another. Being so deeply personal and experiential, the Heart Awakening energy is something that words can allude to, but the full depth of the experience is something they cannot convey. What I am saying is that the force of your original Divine Love within is vastly different from anything that our intellects can understand. When I attempt to express the power of this Love in words, they simply melt back into the vibration of Love. The energy given to me in my own personal revelation of Divine Love that I now call Heart Awakening is the most powerful transformational experience I know. It is so rich, so inspiring, that it feeds the deepest needs of the soul's desire for self-expression and liberation. It answers the deepest prayers of the heart. Without it, life had seemed to me like an ocean of mediocrity.

Helping a person reach this point in their spiritual growth is what has inspired me to do Heart Awakening. Whether you get there by yourself or through a session does not matter. What is important is that you discover the quality of this energy of Divine Love that resides within your inner Self and connect with it so that you can be free. It is at this point when personal power and Divine power become One - a truly surrendered state wherein your ego personality is released and the real You becomes reborn. To touch this nectar and reach this space even once, forever changes all levels of your being. You will never be the same. The seeking for a connection with God, with happiness and perfection, will be over, for you will have learned the secret of who you really are. It is this alignment that allows miraculous healing to occur beyond your comprehension. It happens because you have been willing to give up your attachment to being a body and a personality. Instead you are a Light. You have realigned yourself with the forces of the Divine so that your original Divine love is reflected throughout your energy fields.

Does this happen to everyone in a session? If the genuineness of commitment and desire is there, Spirit always responds. However it is an act of Grace that comes from a continued journey to know the heart of God more profoundly than anything else. It is an act where the accumulated karma of all of the health, relationship and material forces you have ever experienced needs to be reconciled. It happens in its own time, in its own way.

Is it necessary for everyone to go through this? Personally I feel that at one time or another this soul-level reconciliation must be faced by everyone, but the timing, need and intensity vary widely from one person to the next. Why? Because once you discover your own path to freedom, once you rediscover your real Self, you will never feel yourself lacking in the power you need to stop wasting time on things that are not true to your life's purpose in any way ever again. You'll know that whatever you need is yours, because the only thing you will ever want is to be an extension of God's Love. To truly and wholly fulfill our life's purpose is the richest and most rewarding experience we can ever have. So whether it's Heart Awakening or some other path, find your road back to your Self. The inner journey is always the hardest yet the most inevitable, and bears the richest fruit.

PART C
HEART AWAKENING STORIES

CHAPTER 5

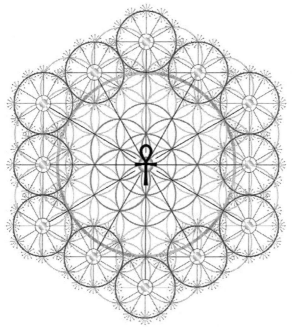

REDISCOVERING YOUR DIVINE CHILD

During a Heart Awakening session, it is not unusual to be taken back to experience the inner divine child because many psychological patterns are rooted in childhood experiences. Releasing the common illusions of this period, when children look outside themselves for love, produces very powerful long-term shifts in perspective.

Peeling Back the Layers

Most of us haven't experienced the freedom of our essence since we were children. As I discussed earlier in this volume, I was born remembering something very important, something essential to my life and its process. I lost that memory at age seven and, although I continued to live in the world, it wasn't until many years later that these precious memories were restored through my own Heart Awakening. The same is true with so many people who come for Heart Awakening sessions. As a child you knew who you were, although that knowing gradually faded as you grew. Those memories still remain within you and will be recaptured when you reopen your heart.

There is a distinct difference between Heart Awakening and other "inner child" therapies. The Heart Awakening session deals more with freeing the true energy of Spirit trapped since childhood rather than trying to intellectually grasp what went wrong during the formative years. The earliest patterns of the ego are set within the dynamics of the child self. Oftentimes these patterns have caused us not to love ourselves.

The essence in each of us is a clear, pure emanation of Divine Love and light. The many thought patterns that created who we believe ourselves to be are attached to that energy and form the basis of your character.

Spirit resides within all levels of your being but the level of energy at which its presence is felt may be closed because of a congestion of thought patterns held since early childhood. These patterns block the unlimited flow of life-force energy and the actualization of your full potential. Releasing these layers is somewhat like peeling an onion. As each layer is peeled off, the true heart energy becomes freer, Spirit reveals itself, forgiveness occurs and the soul is liberated.

A Heart Awakening session, although in part having to do with understanding and clearing childhood issues, has everything to do with the freeing of your true essence. This is what enables you to make long-term changes in your life without having to endlessly analyze your past.

Many times I have seen people who, through therapy or counseling, have "released" a certain pattern on a mental level, yet have not released the pain emotionally.

As a child, Melinda had been severely abused by her father. Although she had gone through many years of traditional and alternative therapies, and intellectually understood what had happened, her life overall was still being negatively affected by her troubled childhood. As I began the energy work with Melinda, I was aware of several areas in her aura that had been significantly damaged due to an energy blockage in the area of her chest stemming from chronically suppressed emotion.

As the session continued, Melinda was gradually directed by her inner self, back to the memories of herself as a child. As she began to relive the memories, long-suppressed emotions began to rise and suddenly exploded into her consciousness - feelings of being so controlled by her father - feelings of hopeless rage, despair and frustration that could hardly be put into words. Understanding wasn't enough - it felt as though her brain could not intellectually process everything she was feeling. As Melinda struggled with these emotions, I could see the psychoenergetic 'tangles' in the energy surrounding her heart. I focused my attention on these areas of congested energy, and began untangling and smoothing out the various energy strands created by the deeply-held fears and anger.

Once these thought forms began to clear, and her electrical fields (or bodies) were realigned with the universal flows of life-force energy, I was able to physically take hold of an amorphous mass of yellowish-brown to black colored energy and maneuver it in such a way that it realigned through her heart chakra. In passing through the heart energies, the mass literally 'exploded' and dissipated. This type of energy mass I call a psychic implant, which can be self-imposed or directed by another. In other words, when a person 'throws' the energies of control and manipulation at another, especially a child, they act in a sense like an energy dagger or implant, which penetrates deeply into the person's electromagnetic fields. If not removed, the wounds created by these 'energy daggers' fester and in turn create psychological disturbances or physical diseases. With Melinda, I saw that this trapped energy, combined with an already existing hole in the electromagnetic field around her heart (a genetic miasm probably stemming from a past life issue with the *masculine principle), would eventually have caused her to develop cancer. As these energies were cleared, Melinda was finally able to let go, and she burst into tears and began speaking out loud to her inner vision of her father, telling him the truth of how she had felt and how he had made it impossible for her to develop and express her own being and her own individuality.*

The conscious expression of her supressed feelings, together with the clearance of the distorted energies created by her childhood struggle, and the realignment of her electrical fields with the natural flow of divine life-force energy, created a comprehensive and profound soul-level healing that would allow Melinda to finally begin living and expressing her true soul personality. After the session, Melinda said that she felt transformed, brighter, lighter, and freer than ever before. As time went on, Melinda discovered that this soul transformation had brought her the true liberation she had been seeking all her life. She was also able to develop a new deeper and far more loving relationship with her son, a relationship that had suffered terribly because of her unresolved issues with her father.

Freeing the divine child within has helped many people reconnect with a part of themselves that had been suppressed most of their lives. Typically, the deep memory of our connection with our divine Source has been lost since childhood. One of the great gifts of a Heart Awakening session is to experience what caused our earliest sense of separation from the Divine so that we can remember what we knew so well as children.

Many times people only remember the difficulties experienced during their childhood. Some don't remember any of it. Heart Awakening sessions help open the memory circuits and allow real feelings to surface from the heart. The energy field created in the session helps you move into a heightened state of consciousness. In this state, it becomes easier to remember what has been buried for so long, and everything is revealed.

Every child looks for love outside itself. For many of us, this is the core pain that can create so much confusion later in life. The love is within, yet so many children are taught that love can only be found outside of self. As a result they cannot distinguish between themselves and others. They grow up continually searching for 'other' love rather than self-love.

The divine child is completely free. It retains full conscious memory of its soul purpose, and does not want or lack anything. Most importantly, it expresses its true nature so well that language is superfluous. I have noticed a lot of inner-child work is based on an on-going need to continue to love the inner child. With the divine child, such a need is gone. The divine child doesn't need love because it knows it is love. When you make the shift to rediscovering your divine child, the ego-based need to heal and love the wounded inner child is gone. The divine child already has and is pure love. When you become the divine child once more, all aspects of the wounded child are healed effortlessly.

When Sarah saw her child-self, there was a sad and miserable expression on her face. The little girl inside felt abandoned, isolated, and stuck, not knowing what to do. As Sarah slowly communicated her thoughts and feelings, it became clear that, as an infant, she had received and felt intense love from her mother, which, as she grew older seemed, for some unknown reason, to fade. Apparently, her mother had felt that an infant was 'easier to love' than an older child who was harder to control. As a result, Sarah had grown up feeling abandoned, and had developed a complex desire to continually discover and invent ways of eliciting the love from her mother that she had felt as an infant. This desire gradually created a manipulative, controlling personality that alienated friends and destroyed her relationships. As the energy work progressed, I saw that this conflict had created a general weakening and depletion of her electromagnetic energies throughout her childhood and into adulthood, which had resulted in an inability to accomplish anything in her life. Her unconscious preoccupation with her need for mother-love and her inability to understand why it had been withdrawn continuously interfered with her development. By the time she had reached adulthood, Sarah felt that she would never be able to understand why her life didn't work, why she felt empty, unfulfilled and couldn't get what she wanted from her life. As Sarah expressed these feelings, I saw that the energies around her crown chakra had been severely affected by her struggle. Because of her unconscious preoccupation with what had happened in her relationship with her mother, an accumulation of psychoenergetic congestion had developed around the left side of her head that was pulling energy away from the rest of her electromagnetic field. She had subconsciously been trying so hard for so long to solve the riddle of what had happened with her mother that it had caused an excess of energy to build up around the left side (the thinking side) of the brain.

This energy field around the crown chakra was so far out of balance, that it had caused her to almost completely lose touch with the underlying issues with her mother, creating a type of psychological 'holding pattern' that prevented her from moving forward with her life. As I worked with this energy field, I found that it began to unravel like a coiled spring, allowing me to actually pull the compacted energy mass apart. As the tightly coiled energy mass unwound, I was able to see the elemental thought forms at the core of the energy coil that were creating the problem. The thought forms were essentially Sarah's unconscious feelings that she could never have what she passionately desired and needed most - her mother's unqualified love. As I gently smoothed out and directed love and energy over the thought forms, Sarah suddenly began to verbally express this unconscious desire and in a flash of conscious recognition, she was able to finally acknowledge the dynamics of what had been occurring in her life up to this time. Tears and an enormous sense of realization and relief flooded over her, helping to clear away the remaining energy mass around the head that had been created from a perception and belief that she had never been able to pinpoint or understand.

This realization allowed her to finally let go of the manipulating, troubled outer self, to melt back into a full resonance with the energies of her true soul identity. She experienced this as a beautiful soft, loving force that suddenly lifted her emotions, replacing them with a powerful electrical charge that ran throughout the cells of her body. She was flushed from head to toe with a newfound exhilaration that allowed her heart to burst wide open. In that instant of deep surrender, Sarah was able to replace her need for love from outside herself with the deep love that God had for her. *Tears streamed down her face as she re-experienced her natural child-like innocence and happiness. She saw her divine child in its essence and felt a tremendous freedom and happiness that brought a whole new youthful expression into her day-to-day life.*

This is an example of how the inner child leads us into a realization of what we are like when we have released the negative aspects of the ego. As we see life from the perspective of the divine child, the duality of life disappears along with any unprocessed emotions.

Healing Childhood Trauma

Sexual child abuse can have serious consequences.

Plagued by a lifetime of failed marriages, loneliness and an ego that believed in controlling others as a way to salvation, Charles was beginning to suspect that something had gone seriously wrong when he was a child. The natural child-like vibration of trust and innocence was something he simply could not get in touch with.

Buried emotional trauma had damaged the flow of energy in his electrical bodies. During the energy work with Charles, I saw intensely 'bunched' fields of energy around his pelvic area. All the energy that should have been flowing smoothly around the legs had accumulated as dense blocks of energy in the pelvis which could eventually have led to prostate problems, lower back pains and digestive distress.

The distorted energies were being pushed up towards the head. This led to Charles' increasing inabilty to understand or get in touch with his emotions (this was probably the source of his Attention Deficit Disorder). When properly channeled, earth forces are extremely powerful and provide an infinite flow of energy that can be used for healing and clearing. A larger than usual concentration of energy was needed to help Charles, so I used the earth forces to unravel his compacted energy block.

As I focused these energies, the negative 'chi' or life-force began to clear, unraveling the locked-up energy strands, and returning the chakras (energy centers through which we focus our consciousness) to their normal directional movement. (Negative chi can cause affected chakras to spin counter-clockwise which can result in chronic negative thinking and attitudes).

This clearance suddenly triggered Charles' suppressed memory of having been sexually molested. Deceived by a relative, his shame and guilt had turned to rage and confusion. For months after the incidents, Charles didn't know who to turn to or what to do. The result was a complete stunting of his ability to express himself emotionally. The deep sense of betrayal and injustice that he experienced weakened his connection to his life-force energy. The result was impotence and failed marriages. Charles had compensated for his extreme emotional distress by constructing a strong, seemingly impenetrable ego and intellect, and drew his personal power from anger and control. The way of holding his energy made Charles' mental body extremely strong, but his feeling and sexual centers became so weak he could hardly get in touch with them. The sexual abuse had been emotionally devastating. It had caused a large tear in the auric energy field that ran from the pubic area to the solar plexus, which needed continual repair work so that he would no longer relive the experience.

With the conclusion of the energy work, enough blocked energy mass had been removed to allow a much more normalized flow of chi through the damaged areas. This for-

*tunately made the emotional release much more rapid and
enjoyable than Charles had thought possible. During the
session, he experienced what it was like to be a trusting
innocent child again, not just intellectually or from memory,
but feeling vibrant, joyful and fulfilled emotionally.*

*By the time he was done he was a radiant beaming child
glowing from ear to ear. In the recovery of his innocence, he
truly understood the meaning of the words, "As a little
child you enter the kingdom of heaven." Rediscovering his
innocence was like being reborn all over again - a firm
believer in love, humility and trust. With his new-found
ability to express his feelings and a rekindling of his sexual
energy he was able to find a mate and enjoy life again.*

Heart Awakening for Children

Quite often, it is appropriate for children to have a
Heart Awakening. Generally they will ask for one
themselves. They are easier to work on than adults.
Sessions can be done for babies and children of any age.
Cleansing the auric field of children is useful in pre-
venting long-term problems from accumulating in the
emotional body. If the child is old enough, there will
still be a breakthrough portion where the child can
"talk with God" and resolve whatever issues are at
hand. Children today are generally conscious of who
they are and what they are here to do. Their sessions
are usually shorter and provide an excellent opportunity for them to discover more about themselves.

*Meg was only fifteen years old when she had a Heart
Awakening session concerning her great fear of being
abused. Her parents certainly weren't abusive to her, so she
recognized that the pattern had to come from somewhere*

beyond her ordinary understanding. Although Meg was unsure about the concept of past lives, her Heart Awakening session did take her back to a previous lifetime during which her husband had sexually abused her. This abuse had led to a self-induced miscarriage in that lifetime.

The guilt and anguish Meg felt about this incident carried over into her present life, creating a fear of abuse. During her Heart Awakening session, the revelations of what had occurred in a prior life experience brought a realization of how much she truly loved herself, and that the fear of abuse she felt was related to energies that could be cleared. In working with Meg, I saw that the energies of her rear solar plexus, head and throat chakras had been damaged by her intense fear reaction to the sexual abuse she had suffered previously. With one hand I slowed down the abnormally fast spin of the chakras, and with the other I cleared the emotional stress that lay between the chakras and the physical body. As the chakras began to slow, by helping Meg deepen her capacity to love, she was able to process emotions of intense fear and shock and to let go of her fear of abuse. This deepened capacity to love allowed Meg to feel safe enough to look clearly and honestly at the underlying issues without reacting hysterically. By the end of the session, the major portion of the trauma had been resolved and Meg was able to continue her life with a deep sense of security, confidence and happiness.

No matter what may be going on in your life, even if you are experiencing seemingly insurmountable problems, a Heart Awakening session can radically change your life by putting you in touch with one of the greatest healing forces that exist - your own inner divine child.

CHAPTER 6

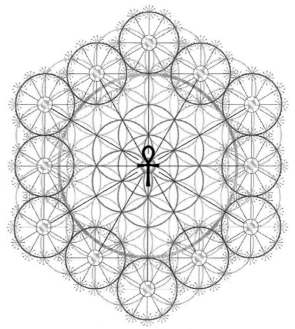

COMPLETING FAMILY
KARMA

Seen from the perspective of the heart, you were born into your particular family to learn key lessons most needed to fulfill your soul's purpose. No matter how difficult or painful your family karma may be, the soul never makes a mistake. The family your soul chose in this life brings to consciousness the core issues you must resolve during this lifetime.

So intent is the soul on fulfilling its purpose, it leaves no stone unturned and every issue brought forward must be resolved. If family issues are not released, they will continue to be played out, endlessly, from one lifetime to another. However, once the family karma is completed, the soul is free to use the personality self as a vehicle to actualize, rather than undermine, the spiritual mission for your life.

Heart Awakening is the most powerful, rapid and effective method possible for the release and resolution of even the deepest and most convoluted family and relationship problems. The sessions connect you directly through your own heart to the divine images of Father and Mother. The ego's perspective, wounded by painful and destructive father/mother relationships, is healed. Once again you are able to perceive and experience the divine Father/Mother/Child relationship and you instantly rediscover your natural, innate ability to relate from the heart. Family and personality issues are dissolved as love and harmony are freely expressed in all your interpersonal relationships.

Experiencing Perfection within Your Family

When you complete your karma with a family member, you feel nothing but incredible Love and compassion for the other person throughout your body, mind and soul. This is quite different from just knowing it intellectually or even being able to say it. When you experience the full impact of a Heart Awakening session, a tremendous energy moves through you and radiates across time and space to those with whom you are working during the session. The expanded heart energy floods Love and completion into a situation wherever the other person may be. Many times people have resolved their karma with a family member and later found that it was also felt by the other person.

Paula felt her life no longer held any value. Raised by an alcoholic father and a heavily dependent and stern mother, Paula needed a series of sessions to sort out her life. As a child, she had been punished and "left for dead" one day, and no one seemed to care. From that day on, she held a deep bitterness and resentment for herself, her life, and her family. She was unable to forgive. When she came to see me, she told me that she had recently discovered lumps in her breasts. She wanted and needed to make major changes.

After a number of sessions concerning her immediate life situation, it was time to deal with her family. To complete family karma, I have found it is necessary to experience the Divine perfection within self as well as each family member. The object of the session is to ask Spirit to help the person see a situation in the way Spirit sees it. Our own perceptions have been limited and biased, but to Spirit there is always a reason for every single thing that happens. Behind every incident and every trauma, there is a message from Spirit that is a gift, even if it is not clearly visible at first.

For Paula, the idea of seeing any kind of perfection or Divinity within her father was repulsive and downright absurd. She had grown up with him, and God was not moving in or around him in any way, shape, or form. But as the session progressed, we gradually peeled off the layers of resentment until she experienced her own perfection. Once she had experienced this, her judgements of her father disappeared. Now she could see the true Spirit personality of her father. There was a great goodness within the man, but he had become trapped. The stress of raising a family had simply exhausted him. As he struggled to provide for his wife and children, he had tried desperately to be positive and to give them hope, but he found that he was emotionally drained and burdened by their unconscious neediness. Although he had actually loved his family very much, Paula's father didn't know how to express his feelings of frustration and anger. As time passed, he had begun to turn these emotions toward his wife and children, not realizing that his anger toward the family was really anger toward himself for not being able to live up to his own expectations as head of the household.

During the session, after the clearing of blocked energies around her solar plexus, Paula saw how her father's soul was fulfilling the purpose of the relationship between them. The stern grip of Paula's fear and rage melted as she began to clearly see what had transpired within her father's heart, and in being able to now understand him, she was able to forgive. She realized, in spite of everything, that Spirit was *working through him and helping her to grow. Although it was never a conscious act, her father had been training her to become independent, courteous, and mindful of the way she spoke. Indeed, these were the qualities her soul wanted to learn. On a personality level, her conscious mind said, "I would never choose a situation like that." But when she saw it through the heart, she was able to forgive, let go, and experience for herself how Spirit had been present throughout her childhood, continually moving her in the direction she most needed to grow.*

When Spirit showed her what was happening, Paula instantly moved into a feeling of tremendous compassion for her father. Her heart opened, and she felt her whole physical body go through a major physiological adjustment as the energy of Spirit moved in and allowed her to feel the true, deep love of her father and of herself.

An Adopted Child and Her Mother

The stories of completing family karma are endless for one reason: the desire for the Love between two people is stronger than the unresolved pattern of the ego. When the soul's hunger for resolution is stronger than the desire to hold on to the pain, Spirit moves in and anything is possible. It is our inherent nature to complete all unresolved relationships and Heart Awakening is a tremendously effective way to do this.

Mary was an adopted child and didn't know where her birth mother was. Thinking she had not wanted her, Mary experienced much guilt and shame. After a series of Heart Awakening sessions on other issues, she decided to have a session regarding her birth mother. As a result, she gained a deep sense of peace within herself about the relationship. As she relaxed into the presence of Spirit's Love, she was able to reach into the deepest part of her inner child self with more sincerity and truth than she had ever expressed before. She turned to God and her mother's soul. She asked with the greatest of humility that whatever she may have done to bring this pain upon herself be forgiven. In a flood of tears, she realized that the separation of her mother's love was the result of a long-held feeling of being separate from God. Finally relieved, she was able to let go and accept a deep sense of peace about her relationship with herself.

Not long after the session, her mother - who had been out of her life for forty-three years - contacted her. Mary was stunned. She had not anticipated Spirit granting her greatest wish: to know her birth mother.

Unmasking the Illusion of Love

Many people think they have completed their family karma and love their family members. But when they get into a session, they discover their forgiveness was only on an intellectual level. Energy clears the most blocked areas of the aura during a session, and the cause of the blockage surfaces to consciousness and reveals what is unresolved. We may think we have forgiven, but in our hearts we haven't. Many of us have never experienced what it is like to forgive. True forgiveness means experiencing through the heart the force of Divine Love. When released, it is a powerful healing force transforming the past and completing karma.

John wanted to be a healer and this was the most important thing in his life. He had read the books and done his

*homework, yet something still wasn't right. He thought he
had been well raised and educated and didn't feel the problems others were experiencing because he came from a "wonderful, loving family."*

*During his session, a different story emerged. Even
though his family had continually expressed love and affection, John was shocked to find it was all just lip service
and he had never truly felt their love and compassion. The
depth of inner plight that this realization created empowered him to go the next step. He aligned himself with pure
intent and allowed the shadow side of his family to be
revealed to the light of Spirit's presence. As he did so, like
a huge coiled spring, the accumulation of lifetimes of manipulation of life-force energy to control others for personal gain
unleashed itself from his energy field. As his body released
the negative emotions, light flooded every cell of his body,
and toxins were dissolved. He felt the incredible joy as that
all-so-familiar flash of light flooded every cell of his body.
He felt the incredible joy of his soul being freed from a pain
so deep he could hardly even describe it. He saw how his
family had the same soul lesson. No wonder the love was so
superficial. They were covering up a fear of the manipulative patterns being discovered. He was free and ecstatic.
The taste of having allowed the light of Spirit's presence
into the darkest corners of his pain gave him a taste of
God's love, vastly greater and infinitely more rewarding
than anything he had ever experienced in his life. Within
that insight lay the key to the problems he was having in
developing his healing practice. He had never deeply connected with the Love within himself or for others that would
guide him as a healer. After one session, with his heart
opened, John was able to move forward in his healing prac-*

tice. He was successful because he now knew what everyone was searching for - a new way to get back to the Love.

Communicating with the Deceased

Many sessions involve completing with a deceased relative. This can be extremely valuable because the issues of love, death and God are often what people need to heal the most. A Heart Awakening session takes you into a heightened state of awareness where you perceive and understand everything on a much deeper level than would otherwise be possible. In this state, working with the angelic realm, you can communicate with a deceased loved one to complete a relationship. The difference between how much a person wants to work on, and how much they are able to work on, is often a key issue in the session. Many dramatic insights can occur because those who have passed on often have a much clearer understanding of their lives and are able to communicate this wisdom to those who are still in the body.

Mary's father had died a year before and she felt deep sorrow because she hadn't been with him before he died. She felt guilty because she knew he wasn't well but didn't want to accept the extent of his illness, and their relationship had been somewhat strained by her inability to acknowledge the seriousness of his condition. Additionally, she had an abandonment issue because her father divorced her mother early in Mary's childhood.

The energy work in the aura allowed an opening within Mary's consciousness that made the task of communicating with her father relatively easy. She found that in the Spirit realm, he looked young, vibrant, joyous and without pain. Together, they resolved the unexpressed issues between them. He asked her forgiveness for all that had happened as a result of his abandoning her as a child. He realized the consequences of his actions and was truly sorry. That was all Mary needed to hear because her feeling of abandonment was the very thing that had hurt her most. This realization also explained why she had refused to be with her father when he died. As they spoke they realized that she had abandoned him in the same way she felt he had abandoned her.

The session was simple, yet profound. It allowed Mary to realize she could never be separated from her father. Their love extended beyond dimensions; whether she was in the body or in spirit, the Love was still present. The Love was a communication channel through which she could always connect with her father. Mary thought she would have to wait until she died to see her father again. Now she realized that was unnecessary because Love knows no time or space. When she was firmly grounded in the body and in her heart, she could expand her awareness through time and space, and connect with her father through Love.

The session also helped Mary make a major adjustment in the way she thought about others. She was the worrying kind, always concerned about how others were doing and what she could do to help them. Seeing her father completely free of pain helped her understand her worrying was unnecessary. The experience brought her a clearer understanding of the infinite love of the Divine Father and of the eternalness of the soul. This helped her be more at ease with her own life process. Mary grew to love herself more and to excel as a portrait artist, selling her cards to many stores all over the country.

Often, when a close relative or loved one has passed away, many unresolved emotional issues are left behind and need to be cleared. Our grief can be so great we don't know what to do with the feelings. A Heart Awakening session provides a safe and unconditionally loving environment where people can freely deal with unresolved issues with those who have passed on.

Rebecca was argumentative with everyone she met. She was no longer able to talk to anyone or go anywhere without fear. She wasn't sure what had happened. During her Heart Awakening session, Rebecca found she had shut down as a child of four when her mother died of leukemia. Rebecca's child self regretted being alive. After her mother's death, Rebecca threw herself headlong into school and her career and never looked back. Now all of this was catching up with her because she had been diagnosed with leukemia herself.

The energy work in the presence of Spirit cleared the energetic pathways so that Rebecca could clearly see and feel herself in the Spirit. As vividly as in 'real life,' she was able to have a conversation with her mother so that she could clear misconceptions about her departure. Rebecca thought her mother left her because she didn't love her. The contrary was true: her mother deeply loved her daughter and bringing Rebecca into the world was the one gift she had given herself. Her joy at having a child was great because she knew she wasn't going to live much longer.

Discovering the truth of what her mother was feeling shook Rebecca. She felt the Love in her mother's voice as she urged Rebecca to recapture the joy of life. She explained much about the Spirit world that helped Rebecca overcome her fear of death. Rebecca promised to change her priorities and savor the God-given gift of life each day. She had tasted the nectar of Divine Love in the physical body and now knew she didn't have to leave the world to gain her mother's love. God's Love was inside her, and it was eternal.

The depth of such a spiritual and emotional shift cannot be underestimated.

Heart Awakening awakens a deep light within you that inspires you to look after yourself until you feel continuous joy in your daily life. This is the true nature of healing.

Releasing Addictions by Loving Yourself

When there are unresolved core issues with a relative, their passing can have a tremendous impact on our lives.

Marie started smoking soon after her father died when she was ten years old. Not long after, she began smoking marijuana as well. Marie was in her mid-forties when she came to see me. Due to her addictions, her health was rapidly deteriorating.

During her Heart Awakening session, Marie discovered she felt responsible for her father's death. He had committed suicide. She felt a great sense of guilt and shame because he had been continuously angry with her for not living up to his expectations. Her father communicated with her from the spirit realm and apologized for the enormous pain his suicide had caused her. He told her the problem had to do with his own deep sense of inadequacy as a father. He had never known how to love himself and had never felt capable of raising a family. As a result, he had been unable to show Marie his own love for her. He had been helping her

out in whatever way he could. This reconnection with her
father inspired Marie on the deepest levels and helped her to
move past the grief she was carrying.

The impact of Marie's resolution with her father
enabled her to give up smoking from that day on.
With continued sessions over the next few months,
she was able to reach a level of self-love that opened
up a whole new way of living.

Forgiving

For most of us, the majority of our emotional
issues come from interactions with parents or spouses
or siblings. To receive the greatest benefit from a
Heart Awakening session, it is important to be
scrupulously honest about how you feel about yourself in relation to your family members. The energy
work allows buried feelings to surface and be
expressed until you are finally able to see and feel
your key relationships from the perspective of Divine
Love. At that moment, the letting go and forgiveness occur on all levels of consciousness: emotional,
mental, physical and spiritual. With your inner
light, your inner love, and your inner power awakened, the liberation of the soul purpose becomes a
physiological life transforming experience.

Through this process, family karma becomes a
thing of the past. You are able to continue your journey through life with loving, nurturing relationships
that reflect the acceptance of the oneness that unites
us all. When a person loves him or herself enough,
they automatically find love, peace and harmony in
all their relationships.

CHAPTER 7

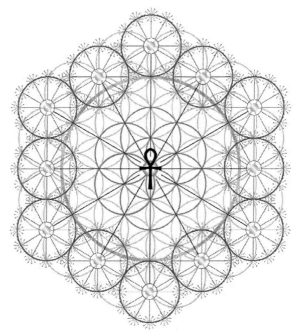

FINDING LOVE IN YOUR
RELATIONSHIPS

The first step in the healing of all relationships comes through learning the difference between "personal attachment" love and Divine Love. The two are very different.

Bringing in a New Relationship

Personal attachment is driven by the ego that seeks to get and forget. Spirit seeks to give and forgive. The function of a Heart Awakening session is to help you gradually replace conditional love, attachment, and dependency with a natural expression of giving and sharing arising from the knowingness of the infinite abundance of Divine Love. Once you learn to follow Spirit's guidance, the joyous, loving relationships your heart has always longed for will be attracted to you. Expressing yourself from Spirit is the key to success in all relationships and Heart Awakening can help you develop that skill.

Julia's life had been difficult. She had had only one lover in her entire life. She had married a man with whom she had a sexually abusive relationship that lasted for twenty-four long and painful years. Although he was now with another woman, she hadn't been able to move on. In spite of the abuse and his other relationship, she hoped he would come back. In reality, this was unlikely.

Going through the Heart Awakening session was difficult for Julia. She resisted any kind of belief in God or spiritual Divine essence. It was foreign and against her beliefs. She was, however, able to recognize the depth of her resistance, which surprised her. She completed the session as best she could and left. In her conscious mind she didn't think the session had done her any good. But Spirit was supporting her heart where she needed to be, supporting the genuineness of her heart's desire, not the negative reactions to the ego personality.

Two weeks later she called, totally ecstatic because she had met a new lover and scheduled a trip to the Bahamas. For Julia, this was a miracle. It helped restore her faith in God and her heart softened. For the first time in many years, she cried, joyous and grateful that her life had finally changed.

Opening to a Long-term Relationship

One of the joys of giving Heart Awakening sessions is the incredible moments shared with people as they journey into themselves. They remember the wisdom of Divine Love and discover the truth of who they are is their beauty, not their pain.

John couldn't keep a relationship for more than six months. All his life he recreated the same pattern. Each time he got close to someone, he became increasingly aware of the other person's faults until he had to leave. He couldn't face himself anymore.

It took a number of sessions for John to let go of his judgment towards women. What was really going on was that he was his own worst critic. The standards he had set for himself for where he wanted to go and what he wanted to do built up an intense, self-directed harshness and he was projecting it onto others. Through Heart Awakening sessions, he gradually released the need to be so exacting with himself. He softened and became much more gracious, kind, and loving. He was then able to draw a long-term, stable relationship into his life because he was able to love himself fully.

Reuniting Couples

Heart Awakening sessions can make the difference between a relationship lasting and not lasting. Often the problem lies in a lack of knowledge about the spiritual principles necessary to make a relationship work or in a shallow perception about how one's own patterns have been projected onto another. One sign a Heart Awakening might be needed is when a relationship has reached an impasse where the partners find they can't go any further, and new insights are necessary to make it work.

I have noticed this occurrence quite often with couples. When one partner comes to a spiritually open, heart-centered life and the other does not, there are likely to be some changes. Ideally, for a relationship to work, both need to be anchored in knowing the Divine Love within themselves.

Claire came in for a session to complete the relationship with her ex-husband. She had to move on from the relationship because she was evolving at an exponential rate spiritually, and he had absolutely no interest in working on himself. It was a difficult choice because she loved him and he loved her, but her path was leading in a different direction.

Two years later, Claire's ex-husband came in for a session. It was time for his inner process to begin. Molested at birth by an abusive parent, he had grown up with a deep sense of guilt and deprivation that led to a poverty consciousness. Bound by the need to keep the family checkbook in balance, he hadn't been able to follow his wife's spiritual quest. His Heart Awakening session transformed his life and for the first time he was able to love himself. His guilt and shame turned into a deep sense of appreciation for himself and his life.

Two weeks later, I received a telephone call. Unexpectedly, the couple had gotten back together. Before her husband's session, Claire couldn't stay in the marriage because he couldn't open his heart. Now his heart was pouring out Love for himself and for life, so they were able to continue their relationship.

Forgiving Renews Marriage Commitment

Terry and Janine had had enough of each other during ten years of marriage, a great deal of which had been spent quarreling. They came independently for sessions to complete and release the other because they were ready to move on.

Both of them understood the importance of completing a relationship, but they didn't understand Spirit's agenda for a relationship. Terry came in first and during the session was able to forgive himself for everything he couldn't resolve in the relationship. The more he forgave, the more he was able to feel Divine Love. The more he got into the Love, the more he realized how his ego had sabotaged what could have been a perfectly good relationship. He discovered that the process of forgiving himself to complete the relationship recreated the Divine Love he and Janine had when they first met. The session shocked him into realizing how valueless their quarreling had been. It inspired him to focus on Divine Love rather than on personality differences.

In Janine's session, she moved through her suppressed feelings and recognized her fear of losing Terry had actually created the loss of the relationship. She forgave him from the deepest parts of herself, recognizing anything unlike Divine Love is illusion and that she had refused to learn from her mistakes. The closer she came to understanding what Spirit intended for her, the more she realized separation from Terry wasn't what Spirit wanted. They needed to stay together, learn the courageous art of forgiveness, and appreciate the good each had to offer the other.

A week later they decided to stay together. Having cleared their unresolved patterns, each felt a much deeper love for the other - they found the Divine Love that had always been present, even though it was covered up by the accumulation of unforgiveness neither knew how to release.

Saving a Marriage

Spirit can dissolve all of the differences in a relationship and leave you with nothing but the Love. The desire for its expression becomes greater than the desire for the differences.

When a healing is offered by Spirit, it is always received by the individual. Sometimes a person might want a Heart Awakening session around a particular issue, but for that to occur, something altogether different might need to happen first.

Arthur and Yolanda were at their wits' end. She had been chronically ill most of her life with just about every ailment known to medical science. She no longer wanted to live and Arthur had had enough. He was exhausted from working around the clock to pay for all the healing necessary to keep her going, even though it was obvious to him she wasn't happy to be alive. The years of stress had erased any self love and their life had no meaning.

Yolanda's session helped her experience the Love within.

It reversed her long-held belief that the true essence of spirituality couldn't be experienced in the body. Once she got through her fears and felt the Love within herself, she felt welcome on earth. She had greatly feared coming to this planet and had never relaxed enough to feel the joy of being incarnate. Her fear of being in the physical body came from past life experiences she recalled in vivid detail. She moved through her feelings of being misunderstood and rejected for all the spiritual work she had done, whether she was in the body or in spirit, and reached a state of acceptance where she felt safe living on earth again. She finally opened to receiving Love from others.

Arthur's session enabled him to soften enough to feel compassion for his wife. He came into the session feeling the situation was impossible and was considering leaving her. But through the eyes of compassion, Arthur found a greater lesson. Spirit was teaching him to serve and open his heart. He had spent all of his adult life focused on the business world and had always avoided the lesson of true compassion. His attitude changed as he found greater virtue in forgiveness and persistence. He found the strength to continue and the session saved their marriage.

There are no shortcuts in the healing process. The energy always goes where it is needed most, even though the ego might think it should go somewhere else. Once the energy is aligned with truth, it has to be followed, and we never really know the destination because the true journey is in what the present moment offers. Sessions unravel what cannot exist in the higher truth. They don't superimpose a new layer on top of the old. They reveal what has been forever and can never be disputed.

Anne wanted to heal her relationship with her husband. As the session progressed, there was a gentle realignment of her personal energy with her soul's energy. As all the cells of her body absorbed the frequencies of Divine Love, Spirit revealed to her the need to complete with her father because she had married a man who resembled him. When she felt the fullness of love that lay between her and her father, she was amazed at the difference it made. Free of her projections, the relationship with her husband took on a whole new perspective. A part of her already knew how much she loved him, but thanks to the energy work, she was able to experience the full force of this love, unhindered by unresolved emotions and the discomforts of a tired physical body.

Welcoming a New Relationship

A full Heart Awakening cannot be sought as an end in itself. In spite of ulterior motives, people who come to sessions still experience the presence of Spirit and the energy into which they are being invited.

Ben heard of the work. He was about to go on his first date with a new girlfriend and thought he could make the most use of it by getting his heart open. He was looking for immediate results without realizing the extent to which his ego needed to surrender. He didn't understand a complete Heart Awakening comes only as a result of a sincere desire to do the inner work and come into full integrity in all areas of life. A full Heart Awakening is a gift from Spirit, the result of a genuine desire to restore Love in all key relationships.

Ben did get an awakening and experienced what the energy was like, but he wasn't ready to receive its full benefits because, as he realized, his motives weren't pure. A

subsequent session, when his motives were clear, produced the
breakthrough he wanted. By experiencing the difference
between Spirit's agenda and the ego's agenda for a relation-
ship, he was able to make the inner shift he needed to settle
into a long-term relationship with his new girlfriend.

Reuniting With A Friend

Clearing the heart means clearing the relationships of
the past and present. Heart Awakening sessions serve as
a reminder of how Spirit works within us to heal anything and everything as long as we are willing to let
Spirit prevail in all our interpersonal relationships.

Tony came to a Heart Awakening group gathering.
Although he had little interest in God or healing, he was
hurting because he had a falling out with his dearest
friend. During his Heart Awakening session at the gather-
ing, he found he could not move through the pain he was
experiencing around this lost relationship. I came over to
the table to help him and felt the energy he was experienc-
ing. All it took were the words, "What does your heart
want to say to your friend?" Suddenly, Spirit moved in,
his heart melted, and Tony was able to express himself with
nothing held back - just a pure genuine expression of what
his heart was feeling. Tony discovered love heals everything
and was able to complete and release the relationship, know-
ing he had done all he could.

Two days later, his friend called, apologizing for the way
he had behaved and planning a trip to visit him. To Tony,
it didn't matter if God existed or not. His genuine desire to
free his heart had brought him a miracle. He realized he
didn't have to understand intellectually how to heal the
relationship. Spirit could come alive within him and give

*him the wisdom to express what was needed to reunite him
with his friend.*

Improving A Work Relationship

Once we realize and accept Spirit's perspective of
our relationships, all interpersonal problems are
healed. The unity that naturally exists within all of
us is infallibly restored. We no longer continue to
magnetize recurring painful relationships in our daily
lives.

*Annette's relationship with her boss was causing prob-
lems in her job. She was the manager of a title company
and was having great difficulty because her boss, a middle
aged man, was harassing her continually. Being a single
mother, she couldn't afford to quit her job.*

*Her session revealed a deep contempt for men in general
and a hatred of their dominant and aggressive nature. As
the session progressed, Annette realized her attitude towards
men was a reflection of deep problems in her relationship
with her father. She perceived him as a very domineering
and controlling individual. The release and forgiveness of
her father that Annette experienced during her Heart
Awakening allowed her to see, despite the pain and difficulties, that her soul had chosen this type of father so she
could develop a more assertive character. During the session,
Annette saw the divine perfection of her father and spoke to
him from her heart about how she felt. She realized repress-
ing her anger towards her father had built up resentment
that colored her attitude towards all men.*

After her Heart Awakening session, Annette's relationship with her boss improved tremendously. All
the harassment stopped because Annette was no

longer "harassable."

Completing Old Relationships

One of the most useful times to have a Heart
Awakening session is after the break-up of a relationship. Sessions leave no place for the ego to hide.
Any unresolved aspect of a relationship can be clearly
felt in the aura. There can be no lying to self, saying
a relationship is resolved when it is really not. The
incredible power and radiance of a vibrant open heart
is unmistakable. When there is completion in a relationship, all you can remember about the other is the
Love, unconditional and unattached. That only
comes when everything Spirit was trying to teach
during the relationship has been learned. Then you
experience true peace.

*Sally had just ended a six-year relationship with her
husband. She was feeling shaky and uncertain. The marriage had been difficult because she couldn't communicate
her needs and feelings to her husband. The gap between
them grew wider until it became irreconcilable, leaving her
feeling incomplete. Several months after the breakup,
although she was focusing her mind on other things, Sally
still felt deeply hurt emotionally. She believed she could not
open up to another relationship in the future.*

*The Heart Awakening session brought Sally the closure
she needed. She saw her husband in his perfection and
released a part of herself she recognized had been a major
part of the problem. Since childhood she had held onto a
great sense of neediness in her relationships with others.
Sally saw how this neediness had alienated her husband.
She had been too demanding, thereby pushing him away.*

97

She also had a great deal of trouble because he seemed to be attracted to her only sexually and not on a true heart level. Much to her surprise, Sally discovered during the session she had developed the attitude that "men are only interested in sex" in her teens. She had drawn that type of person because, deep within herself, she believed "all men were alike."

The real revelation for Sally was the discovery of the quality of energy and the attitude she needed to develop in order to receive the grace of Spirit's healing power.

This realization allowed a major breakthrough and she began to forgive both herself and her husband. Sally saw the Love had been there, but he hadn't been able to get through to her because of her own limited experience of how to work with Spirit. By the end of the session she had released a deep feeling of not deserving someone who was right for her and, inspired by her new-found partnership with Spirit, felt ready to meet the next loving relationship.

Settling Divorce Proceedings

Spirit never upholds a feud between two people. There is always a perception and an understanding through which differences can be dissolved. A court fight often signifies anger and hate of self has been focused onto the other person. When the forgiveness and the lesson have been learned, the battle is over.

Melissa's life had an unexpected twist. After twenty-three years of marriage, her alcoholic husband had beaten her up, leaving her partially paralyzed and barely able to walk. The anger and bitterness between the two of them had manifested physically. She was in the middle of divorce proceedings primarily centered around her belief she was permanently disabled and should be awarded permanent disability pay from him.

Her husband, on the other hand, adamantly claimed, "You aren't paralyzed. You can walk fine. You don't need the money." To Melissa's outer mind, he was in insane denial of reality. She was doing everything she could with her lawyer to fight the case.

During her Heart Awakening session, we looked at the situation through her heart with Spirit's perception. Melissa discovered by insisting on permanent disability pay, she was in effect telling herself she would be permanently disabled. She already knew the principle of the power of thought in creating our perception of reality. She was in the process of identifying herself as being permanently disabled - a self-image she could have carried for the rest of her life. Paradoxically, she saw Spirit was working through her alcoholic husband, telling her not to accept herself as disabled. By realizing this, Melissa was able to forgive her husband on the deepest level. After her session, she chose to readjust the way she approached the divorce proceedings and simply asked for enough money to allow her the time to heal herself over the next few years.

Forgiving a Deceitful Husband

Co-creating with the Divine is realizing the only true marriage is the union of the soul with its Divine essence. This relationship provides the permanent perfect romance. It never lets you down, never abandons you, never betrays you or deceives you, and never, ever stops loving you, no matter what you do.

That is why it is so critical for us to be aware of how the soul communes with the Divine, enveloped in the ultimate romance. Heart Awakening's purpose is to help all of us gain this awareness and "live happily ever after."

Having recently moved to Phoenix with her newlywed husband, Maggie discovered he was involved in illicit affairs. Completely shocked, she couldn't condone what he was doing and her life turned upside down. She believed herself happily married, only to find her life was based on a stunning illusion. A Heart Awakening session revealed the spiritual lesson behind the situation for her. Her need to marry for money had blinded her from seeing the truth.

The session opened her up to the Divine perspective and allowed her to see the whole situation through her heart. Doing this meant letting go of blaming her husband for deceiving and betraying her. It meant releasing her attachment to the fight over finances to receive a higher gift - the capacity to co-create her life in partnership with the Divine, thereby gaining access to all the abundance she wanted.

Having forgiven herself and her husband, she was open to understanding how a financial settlement could be reached that didn't require her to sacrifice her integrity or her heart.

Dissolving Breast Lumps

Usually we don't consciously recognize how much unresolved emotional baggage is left after a broken relationship. Often it gets buried, sometimes so deeply that physical symptoms, like lumps in the breast, can occur.

Judy had built a strong wall of irreconcilable patterns within her marriage. Unable to reach a resolution, she and her husband divorced without resolving the underlying issues responsible for the problems. Three years after the divorce, Judy discovered lumps in her breast. She knew they were related to the repressed emotions surrounding the marriage, but was unable to find a way to release these physically devastating issues.

By the time she came to see me, the repressed pain and hatred she felt for her ex-husband were so deep it took a number of Heart Awakening sessions to get through the layers. When the real emotions surfaced, she realized her true feelings of hatred were due to having devoted so much time to her ex-husband without receiving any nurturing in return.

In the natural flow of the energies, the feeling of hate was released from her heart freeing her from the deeply repressed emotions towards her ex-husband. This did not require in-depth mental analysis or the identification of specific beliefs. Rather the session gave her the opportunity to experience how Spirit could convert her negative emotions into unconditional love for herself and her husband.

The lumps in her breast were gone the day after the last session. When I spoke to her six months later, the lumps had not returned.

Resolving a Divorce

Spirit's perspective within a relationship is more about resolving differences and coming into the heart than with creating separation. When the ego has said "enough," there is usually an important lesson to be learned. Often what surfaces is the core pattern most needing release. We tend to break off a relationship when things get rough because the ego thinks ending the relationship will solve the problem. Whether the relationship is continued or completed, Spirit's intention is for the two people involved to experience unconditional Love for one another. The desire to end a relationship is a function of not being able to see or understand the issues being reflected. The willingness to look at what is creating the desire to separate is actually a great gift and an opportunity for self-healing. If not taken advantage of, it will trigger more relationship problems in the future.

Denise had been married for thirty-four years but had finally decided to get a divorce and move to Phoenix. Still filled with hate and anger from all that had transpired during the marriage, she came to Heart Awakening for resolution. As she moved through her session, she saw the greed and financial power her husband had wielded in the marriage had been a tremendous threat to her. Despite her unhappiness, insecurity had caused her to hold on to the marriage long after she realized it was never going to work. The anger and hate she had toward her husband were really the anger and hate she had toward herself for not having the courage to step out into the world and develop a career of her own. As a result of the session, Denise saw the perfection of her husband as the aspect of herself that needed to learn how to handle her affairs in the material world. She finally saw the relationship the way Spirit had always wanted her to see it.

The moment that insight occurred, she couldn't hold on to the resentment, and the battle between them was over. Everything was confirmed in her mind when he came to visit her to sort out the divorce arrangements. What Denise expected to be a long drawn-out battle became much easier. She no longer tried to get from him what wasn't hers. The offer she received was fair, and she was free to move on.

Setting a Daughter Free

Even though we come to Heart Awakening sessions to heal all kinds of relationships, we are really healing the relationship with ourselves that is mirrored by another person. When we view all relationships from the perspective that each of us is God, and respond to each relationship as though we are responding to the Divine, healing begins. The ego thinks it can get away with seeing people as less than Divine, and the price it pays is further separation from the Love within. Heart Awakening is about learning to make choices from the heart. In truth, it is the most natural thing in the world.

The greatest challenge in living a heart-centered life for Lana was her daughter's patterns of rebellious behavior. Lana's Heart Awakening session took her back to her own childhood and the depth of unresolved pain she had experienced with her mother. Feeling unloved and misunderstood, Lana had acted out the same rebellious behavior towards her mother that she had been observing in her own daughter.

But what Lana couldn't understand was why her daughter was being rebellious at all. From Lana's perspective, her daughter was receiving an abundance of love and nurturing. During her Heart Awakening session, Lana realized, despite her best efforts to love her daughter, she was subconsciously projecting her negative feelings for her mother onto her. What was disturbing her so much was that she was raising her daughter to be like her mother and herself. When she was able to see her mother, herself and her daughter in Divine perfection, she experienced a major shift in consciousness and forgave her mother and herself for what happened between them.

Her Heart Awakening session set her heart free and she became more mindful of the way she thought of and spoke to her daughter.

Lana experienced the breaking of an endless karmic cycle handed down from one generation to the next. She recognized the importance of her role in putting an end to projecting into succeeding generations the pain and difficulty she had been unable to recognize and resolve within herself.

CHAPTER 8

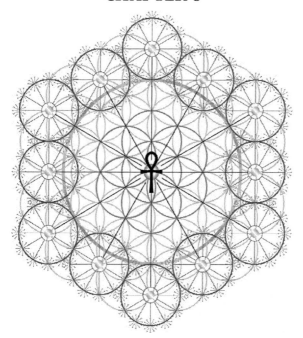

RESTORING
PHYSICAL WHOLENESS

All health problems are the accumulation of thought patterns born of the belief we are separate from Divine love. It does not matter how complex our health issues may appear to be. They all stem from the same cause: the accumulation of beliefs that we are not the whole Divine beings God intended when he created us.

Living with Cancer in Remission

All healing is instantaneous. The only reason we feel it takes time is simply because our personality selves are programmed to believe healing is a long-term process. This belief prevents the personality self from fully accepting our natural inherent Divine nature, which is eternally well and whole.

Heart Awakening sessions create the time and space to allow our personality self to let go of identification with the illusion of separateness from Divine reality. During Heart Awakening, once the personality self realizes all illness or injury is caused by the illusion of separation from your God Self, instantaneous healing can occur on all levels of our being - physical, emotional, mental, and spiritual.

Phyllis was dealing with cancer when she came for a Heart Awakening session. Faced with the incredible turmoil of her life-threatening condition, she was barely capable of expressing her feelings about what was going on. During the breakthrough portion of her session she eventually came to the harsh realization that she had absolutely no control over her life. From the depth of her soul, for the first time ever, she completely turned her life over to Spirit.

A mass of light flooded every cell of her being. It was a challenge for her to articulate and release what she was feeling, but she did as much as she could. A few days later on the plane home, she experienced a spontaneous emotional release. It lasted about twenty minutes. She burst into a wave of tears without understanding why. She just knew to let go. It felt right, and she felt much better about herself afterwards.

It isn't always necessary to know what an emotional release is all about. Releasing the emotion during the session was too much of a jump for Phyllis. It was too deep and personal, yet the intent of the session was fulfilled as soon as she had gotten herself out of the way, when she was ready to receive it.

A few days after Phyllis returned home, she had a physical checkup. Her doctor told her the liver cancer was no longer present.

Family Love Heals Prostate Cancer

One of the most important things we must realize about physical healing is that the body itself has no ability to heal. Spirit gives our bodies life, vitality and health. Without Spirit, the body is simply inert flesh, a fact our personality selves often forget. We fall into the illusion that we are somehow our bodies. This loss of perspective leads us into thinking things like "I'm sick", " I'm weak and frail", "I have cancer", "I'm too old", "body building gives me incredible strength", "jogging makes me healthy". While these statements are true from the ego's perspective, in reality our physical health and vitality are determined through our relationship with Spirit. In a session we open the proper portals in the body to help a person let go of toxic medication from their organs. This has far reaching consequences.

Julius had prostate cancer and was having tremendous difficulties with his family. His Heart Awakening session revealed the true cause of his cancer was his inability to receive love from anyone on any level. Bathed in a field of perfect love, he had the opportunity to look deep inside himself and scrutinize his motives as he went through the core of his inner battle. Was he really going to let the forces of anger and insecurity prevail over the forces of love? Could his soul really live with such a decision? How long could he continue to live with himself without making the change that he knew he had to make? The field of pure loving energies brought into sharp contrast the difference between where he was and where he needed to be. At first he was resistant. He had never been able to do this by himself. Could he do it now? The shift he needed to make was to reverse all of his personality's favorite holding patterns in one go. This seemed an impossible task to his linear-thinking mind yet somehow he knew this could happen by experiencing a depth of self-love so solid and profound that he could recommit to the truth of its expression with all of his heart, mind and soul. His life depended on it. As the objections of the dysfunctional part of his personality were dissolved he was finally able to wholly align himself to accept the love from his family. A flood of energy rushed in, opened the correct portal in his body and removed toxic medical chemicals. An incredible burst of pure radiant love came pouring out of his heart. For the first time in his life, he experienced what it was like to feel the true liberation of his soul. He was no longer worried about being a victim of his cancer. What now inspired him was to get healthy so that he could discover how much more of this love it was possible to know. Feeling the boost of love and appreciation within himself is what gave Julius the resolve to free himself of his illness. The session opened Julius to accepting from his family all the love they had extended his way that he had rejected.

Six months later he came back in, without the cancer, knowing the deep sense of self-love opened within him is what had made it possible for him to heal.

Sometimes it feels the task of reconnecting to Spirit is so huge and overwhelming, it must require lifetimes of striving and struggling. Actually, the reconnection is simple and effortless and takes place in the blink of an eye when you let your mind become one with the heart of God.

The energy work done during a Heart Awakening session contains the pure, raw potential for instantaneous healing. It is the energy of Divine Love and it makes the heart sing. It reawakens our awareness of our Divine Selves, deeply, completely and without years of struggle and pain. Physical healing occurs within this energy field to whatever degree a person can accept.

I do want to emphasize Heart Awakening is a spiritual healing process. When we approach healing from the spiritual level, we make the choice to put our souls in charge. Even though the personality may desire the healing of physical symptoms, the soul may or may not select physical healing as the priority. It may direct its focus to underlying problems in the emotional, mental or spiritual body.

The personality must surrender its desire or demands for physical healing and allow the soul to direct its infinite love, wisdom and healing power where it is needed most. When physical healing occurs, it is because the healing is needed by the soul to complete its purpose on earth.

Although the ego is usually focused on physical well-being as the highest priority, the soul often uses illness or injury to convey a lesson or message to the ego. Once the ego, or personality self, "gets the message" and the physical problem is no longer needed by the soul as a vehicle, the disease or injury simply disappears.

Clearing Buried Emotions Heals Physical Pain

One of the greatest causes of physical disease is the accumulation of worries and fears. These emotions build chronic blockages within the psychic- kinetic and electromagnetic fields surrounding the body. Once cleared, our natural ability to see the Divine perfection within all things is restored. A Heart Awakening session gently unravels the energetic and psychological stress patterns causing physical illness. As the suppressed energy is released, memories of incidents surface and are dissolved, allowing Divine Love in to reveal the illusion of each negative thought pattern. Once this pattern has been dissolved, it can no longer be re-created and the body is free to heal.

When Kim came for a Heart Awakening session, a painful fungus had ravaged one of her feet. As a result of the intuitive counseling portion, we determined that the best thing for her to do was to hold a light but firm intention to stay in a child-like innocence that carried with it a true knowing of what it would be like if she were healed. The rest was up to Spirit. The energy work then provided the realignment and adjustments to her energy field so that there was a sufficient build of psychic-kinetic and electromagnetic energy to effect the healing. During the breakthrough portion of the session, she went into her heart and found herself a child of ten trapped alone in a dark room. Kim remembered how she had put herself there following her mother's refusal to let her play with certain friends. At that instant, she had decided to bury her heart permanently. With the air filled with Spirit's presence, Kim's child gradually came out of the dark room. When her sweet innocent child-self finally revealed itself to the light, a massive jolt of energy shot into her right foot, bringing the life-force energy back into it. The next day her foot was almost completely healed and a few days later returned to normal.

Freeing Yourself from Smoking

The first step on our journey home to Spirit is to master our physical appetites and free ourselves from controlling substances that pull us further into the material world. The early stages of Heart Awakening work might involve giving up smoking, addictive foods or drugs. Clearing accumulated toxins from the aura can make it much easier to let go of addictions.

Jasmine was a smoker for twenty-five years and came in for a Heart Awakening to help her quit. During her session, Spirit gave her a gift. Her lack of self-worth was replaced with an incredible heart-opening experience that allowed her to feel how much God really valued her. The Divine energies poured in, replacing her craving for cigarettes with an infusion of life-force energy. The energy permeated through her lungs and solar plexus, replacing her addiction with a desire to be filled with the essence of the Divine. Jasmine completely quit smoking, and her entire life in general took a dramatic turn for the better.

Heart Awakening is a two-way street. Spirit is always willing to work with you, as long as you are ready to put forward the effort to work with Spirit.

For newcomers to the spiritual healing arts, it may take a little longer to appreciate the full meaning and profundity of Heart Awakening. However, with time and sincere effort, anyone can come to know and experience the enormous benefits and bliss of a Heart Awakened life.

Clearing Recurrent Headaches

It is important to understand the physical body can become a repository for the accumulation of life's unwanted thought patterns. All physical ailments are born in the etheric before they become physical. The physical problem is a clear reflection of the congested thought patterns that need to be released.

Most people are unaware of their auras but are aware of the aches and pains in their body. Around each area of physical pain or discomfort is a field of energy. The aura is a representation of how we have used our energy. For example, the liver might have an auric emanation a few inches or a few feet into the electromagnetic field containing all the memory imprints and impulses of our anger. Or above the chest might be an emanation revealing the stored grief in the lungs. This type of energy sits in the electromagnetic field until it is dissolved. The problem is, most people don't know how to dissolve these energy fields appropriately. Going through an old grief over and over again by kicking a pillow or having a good cry doesn't work. Such actions only cause more anger or grief toxins to build in the energy field, making the situation worse. There is a major difference when release comes as a result of accepting Divine Love, guidance and healing.

The universal life-force energy should flow freely in and out of the seven major chakras and twenty-two minor chakras within the physical body. All aches and pains can be healed through the opening and balancing of the chakras. Heart Awakening gradually releases the emotional patterns that block the chakras, allowing them to open and the energies to flow freely into the physical body. When these energies flow into the seven chakras (or seven seals, as they are referred to in the Bible), the universal energy flows into the corresponding glands. The body is re-energized and revitalized. Our electromagnetic energy field is connected to the universal life-force energy, so our energy can become abundant and pure once these centers are opened and cleared.

Samantha was prompted to come for a Heart Awakening session because of recurrent migraine headaches. During her session Spirit revealed that her headaches were due to her pattern of endless worrying which was causing energy to

"bunch up" in the head. I found an energy leak in her elec-
tromagnetic field above her left ear and a mass of accumu-
lated negative energy around her head. A discarnate entity
had gotten lodged behind the left ear lobe. The session
guided Samantha through layers of emotional congestion
until she released a deep-seated fear of not being good
enough. This core fear was so strong it caused her to worry
constantly about what to do with her life and how to do it.
The Heart Awakening enabled Samantha to re-experience
the wholeness of her Divine Self. This released the entity,
dissolved the congestion of energy around her head and
helped her find a deep sense of inner peace. Following the
session, her headaches disappeared completely and perma-
nently.

Healing Brain Damage

Physical symptoms help point to a different way of
perceiving life. They serve as guideposts to release
old emotional patterns, stay focused in the higher
intuitive centers, and help us learn to live in a state
of harmony and balance. From a psycho-energetic
point of view, physical symptoms are an outward sign
of our overall attitude toward life, which is reflected
as a fixed pattern within the electromagnetic energy
field. Heart Awakening sessions help dissolve these
compositions of thoughts and feelings. After a session, the rigid molding of the personality ego that
binds the soul to the physical plane is loosened and
cracked and gives way to a truer expression of self.
The breakdown of our old attitudes toward life and
the rebuilding of our psycho-energetic perspective on
life allow the aches and pains to disappear perma-

nently.

Denise felt she would carry her cerebral palsy for life. She wanted to focus on what seemed a more immediate problem: she no longer wanted to work as a nurse in a hospital. We discussed the possibility of going to a much deeper level than her mind could accept, recognizing how much her soul really wanted resolution to what was going on physically. (In Heart Awakening it is the alignment of the heart's desire instead of the head's desire for healing that gives it all of its punch and power.) She agreed, and went onto the table with the pure intention to be grateful for the highest level of healing that Spirit could provide.

The energy work revealed numerous tears in the aura, making it impossible to use her life-force energy in a healthy manner. Changing jobs was not going to solve the problem. Repairing the damage done in the energy field above the third eye allowed Denise to see into herself, where the memories of how to heal herself lay dormant.

As the energy work in her aura progressed, Denise was taken back into a vivid memory of herself in the womb with a twin sister who wasn't going to live. Denise felt her intense, complete fear and sorrow about losing her sister and remembered not wanting to continue the incarnation by herself. By the time of her birth, she was terrified of living without her twin. While reliving the experience of her birth, Denise suddenly found herself frozen with fear and unable to breathe. This was what had caused the shortage of oxygen resulting in damage to her brain.

Denise felt the energy flood through her system, releasing the pain of the trauma, and realized she had resolved the greatest mystery of her life - the reason for her physical condition. By the end of the session, she felt in her heart that complete healing in this lifetime was inevitable. More importantly, she felt the greatest impediment to her life had been healed. There was still a great deal to do to strengthen and maintain the realignment of the energy centers around the brain, but the session had released the core impact of the trauma from her electromagnetic energy field. With this done, many possibilities opened up for her and after her session she experienced significant physical improvement.

Clearing A Heart Murmur

Generally there are imprints in the aura that need clearing so we can live in proper balance and harmony. Healing these tangles is important because the Divine energies flow through a balanced electromagnetic field. A single session can be the end to a longstanding physical problem.

Melinda was troubled by a heart murmur and felt there was some psychological reason behind it. Her session revealed a large tear in the spiritual layers above the heart chakra. This tear in the aura was caused by Melinda always looking for love outside of herself and withdrawing her consciousness from her inner heart, depleting it and causing the heart murmur.

The damage to the auric layers was also caused by excessive misuse of her life-force energy to manipulate others in an attempt to obtain love from the outside. The auric damage was repaired on an energy level as she released the core issue underlying the problem. When speaking with her over a year later, she had had no recurrence of the heart murmur.

Healing Chest Pain

The body simply reflects what is going on in a

person's inner and outer life. The more blockages that are released, the easier it is for our souls to direct healing energy to those areas of our being that need it most.

Dennis, a psychologist, had severe pain in his chest for many years. Unable to work, he had exhausted everything he could find in the medical and holistic fields. A Heart Awakening session revealed a frozen mass of energy above the solar plexus chakra. This constriction, an accumulation of fear, had caused a major contraction in some layers of his aura. Each time Dennis tried to do anything, the universal energies flowing through him reached the congealed mass in the solar plexus and caused more pain in the chest, incapacitating him.

The session revealed Dennis had been separated from his mother at birth because of a serious illness that befell her. Left in an orphanage for the first six months of his life, Dennis experienced an enormous sense of loss and grief that was now manifesting physically as intense chest pain. The repair work in the aura allowed the release of Dennis' old fears. Once the effects of the trauma were dissolved and the aura cleared, Dennis found a much deeper level of peace within himself and the chest pain disappeared.

CHAPTER 9

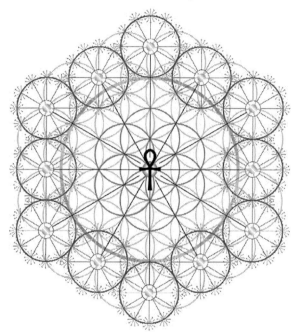

ACCEPTING EMOTIONAL
WELL-BEING

The release of deeply held emotional patterns is perhaps one of the most rewarding gifts you can give to yourself. The soul's desire to be free is so great your simple willingness to be open to change is all you need. When negative emotional patterns have surfaced, been dealt with, and eliminated, there is a tremendous freeing of the heart. Returning to your Divine Self motivates you to change your actions and frees you to live and work with a deep joy and unconditional love for life. The virtues of spiritual wisdom come alive. You feel a renewed sense of enthusiasm, a growing desire to serve and heal, and are constantly replenished by Spirit. To look into Self and feel emotional peace and serenity is a whole new way of living.

The ego is strongly identified with emotions and each time a thought is created and energized through desire, it becomes a positive or negative emotion. Unless something is done to dissolve the elemental life created around each emotion, the related thought pattern continues until it dominates your life or is released.

Heart Awakening was created as a bridge between therapy and spirituality. Unlike traditional therapy, Heart Awakening isn't concerned with analyzing all that happened in your life to justify the problems you are facing. It is concerned with clearing energetic blockages born of the belief in separation from God, so you are free to be your true Self once again.

Releasing Repetitive Patterns

Heart Awakening sessions offer answers to life's most puzzling questions. They open up the capacity to remember as well the ability to restore Divine perception into any situation. What really happened between my uncle and me when I was a child? What happened when my mother adopted my brother? Traumatic moments in a person's life can indefinitely arrest our growth and development, because we become "frozen in time" around dramatic issues. Heart Awakening releases those parts of our personality selves that have frozen the universal life-force energy due to our inability to perceive situations from Spirit's perspective.

Carmen was a schoolteacher working with children in their early teens. Although she found great reward in her teaching, Carmen felt isolated and alone in her spiritual life. She had been unable to find a lasting marriage or love relationship.

During her Heart Awakening session, Carmen found she was inhibited about relating to men because she had experienced many abusive relationships with men in several past lives. She developed the desire to "be a kid" forever during this lifetime to avoid puberty, which triggered the painful memories of abuse and pain surrounding her male relationships. This decision made it impossible for her to develop into a mature adult, thereby short-circuiting her desire for a loving marriage and home. She subconsciously gravitated toward teaching teenagers to resolve this deep underlying issue.

Once Carmen gained this awareness, her heart opened and the "frozen" energy melted, releasing the trauma. A few weeks after Carmen's Heart Awakening, she joyfully reported she had found a boyfriend and was enthusiastically moving forward into her new-found maturity.

Dissolving Anger

Even the most traumatic and heavily charged emotional issues can be released in a gentle, calm and soothing way when enveloped in the Heart Awakening energy of pure Divine Love.

Anna flew in from Chicago for a Heart Awakening session in an effort to find a way to handle her anger and uncontrollable emotional outbursts. She was also having chronic digestive problems. During her session, a large congealed mass of energy sitting directly over her liver was discovered. The mass was her suppressed anger.

As the work proceeded, the accumulated negative charge around the mass began to dissipate until there was nothing but a thin, intense veil of energy across her lower abdomen. When we entered the breakthrough portion of the session, Spirit prompted me to ask: "What did your father do to you as a child to make you so angry?" Ordinarily, such a question might have produced an analytical response of all the reasons why he didn't love her. But the Heart Awakening released the energy behind the thought patterns in her aura until only the true feelings surfaced. In one single outburst, Anna remembered how she had vowed to hate her father for the rest of her life for having scolded her relentlessly as a child.

During her session, Anna recognized how much she actually loved her father. By accepting his human frailties, she could once again feel the love that actually did exist between her father and herself. In expressing the feelings buried in her heart for so long, Anna's anger dissolved and melted away.

Healing Depression

My American Indian teacher once told me if we fail to connect to Divine Love, it turns to fear and affects our emotions. If we fail to express and release our fear, it turns to anger and affects the mind. If the anger cannot be resolved, it turns to grief and affects the physical body. When the grief is unresolved, it becomes depression and affects our spiritual life. It all comes back to the Love not being expressed or shared. The further away from the Love we get, the more of a spiritual problem we have.

Bill came from New Hampshire for his session. Successful by modern day standards as a well-established stockbroker, he nevertheless felt his life was coming to an end. He had accomplished everything he wanted on a material level and couldn't understand why nothing interested him any more. He was going deeper and deeper into an emotional depression.

Basically, Bill's personality self had evolved as far as it could in the outer world, and Bill was ready to allow his soul to begin its inner work on earth. During his session, Bill reconnected to the experience of Divine Love, freeing him from the hopelessness and despair of his materially centered outer life. Once he realized he was free to express and experience the fullness of true Love, his joy of living returned and he saw his life with a renewed, revitalized sense of purpose. His depression turned into inspiration. He was inspired to do healing work, something he had always thought about but couldn't understand, never having felt a connection with the Divine. The commitment to serve gave him the emotional peace he had always sought.

The Healing Magic of Humor

Some people come for a session because they have given up all hope of ever being able to enjoy life.

Jack was referred for a session and it was obvious he was contemplating suicide. His time in the construction business resulted in physical injuries and he spent several years almost incapable of doing anything. He was preoccupied with doubts and fears and had ceased enjoying life in any way. Heart Awakening was his last hope.

In Jack's session, humor was the magic ingredient that broke the ice. Spirit revealed his life from a point of view where all he could do was laugh. Each time he fell into his issues, he was shown the absurdity of having held onto them for so long. As each layer came up, he laughed even harder. He spent the best part of an hour on the table in hysterics. Spirit had shown him the cosmic joke of his life and his worries. He had been tripping over himself again and again and oh, how seriously he had taken it all! By the end of his session, Jack knew the absurdity of taking himself so seriously. Whenever he laughed, major cords and tangles within his electromagnetic field broke up. It was funny, but at the same time, miraculous. No feat of engineering could have repaired his aura the way the energy did that day and all it took was a new perception to turn him around.

Restoring Self Love

We all want to have an open heart. Indeed, every action is a function of our desire to return to unconditional love. But for most of us, this is an unconscious process. We aren't aware of the deeper matters of the inner self. Yet, when this simple aim is recognized and aligned, all the prophesied gifts of Spirit are brought into full experience.

When Rosa called for a session, it was with reservations. In fact, it took her three months to make the decision to come. A part of her knew a session could provide the awareness she had been searching for, but it took that long to prepare herself. Her ego personality knew some major change would take place, and it didn't like the idea. It had become used to complaining, resisting, judging and feeling victimized, and thought it could avoid the session, but her soul knew everything had to be brought into integrity within herself to fulfill her soul's purpose for this life. All the parts of her acting out of fear and desperation were threatened. She thought she could get away with behaving this way forever, but another part of her was stirring, saying, "Look at what is happening. Surely part of you is aware God didn't create a world where you are intended to suffer."

Rosa arrived for her Heart Awakening session ready to give up on life. She was experiencing deep depression about herself, her family, her career, and her health. She couldn't find any meaning in anything she was doing, but by all appearances, her background was solid. She had a good college education and an excellent reputation as an interior designer. But now, everything in her field she had thought held value wasn't there. Family quarrels had been building and she wasn't able to resolve differences with her husband. She was tired, had no energy, and everything seemed an arduous task without reward.

In the early part of her session, Rosa resisted tooth and nail, mostly because of the suppressed anger and hostility she carried toward her father. As the suppressed feelings surfaced during the breakthrough, she discovered how a partic-

ular part of her childhood had affected her ability to feel any kind of love. Once this was revealed, Rosa was free as never before and the pain across her chest was gone. She realized the pain was all about suppressed love and her inability to express it appropriately. It had sent her life down a spiral of missed opportunities and distorted motives.

The session also revealed that Rosa felt horrible because she behaved in a way separate from the Love within. As a result, she couldn't find the purpose in anything. During her session, she recognized her life's purpose was to be the expression of the creative wisdom born of the heart. Each time she followed her heart, her life would flow. Each time she followed the dictates of the outer mind, she would separate from the Love. In the heart, life made sense and had purpose and meaning. Her session revealed the pull between the dictates of the heart and the dictates of the ego personality. Her work was to surrender the parts in fear and make the continuous, moment-to-moment choice of coming from the heart.

Rosa was given a great gift. Her genuine willingness to come into integrity with herself made all this possible. She reached a point where her ego self had nowhere to go, no solutions and was completely lost. The pain and suffering made her ready to allow Spirit to show her life as Spirit would have her see it, through the heart. It was here Rosa realized the depth to which she could feel compassion for her fellow man and make choices from her soul rather than from the dictates of the ego.

Her prayers were answered. Rosa never thought it was possible to feel so much love or freedom within herself. Indeed, she hadn't felt this way since childhood - free in the body and at one with the world and everyone in it. Nothing mattered except the sanctity and purity of the Love within.

Because she could feel the Love inside again, she could make decisions based on her inner guidance that allowed for the expansion of her true self. She experienced the Love so deeply, it was all she wanted to live her life by. Rosa was amazed at how long she had gone without feeling the Love within herself. Intellectually, a part of her knew she "loved" her husband, "loved" her work, "loved" herself, but she had never felt the Love so profoundly as she did that day.

The impact of experiencing herself in her perfection was one of the keys that made the session powerful for her. Although she had spent many years in therapy, Rosa had never been able to get to her core essence. She heard people talk about it, she read about it in many different spiritual teachings, but she never was able to experience the real sacred essence within. She felt as though she had been given the greatest gift in the world. Rosa played, laughed, sang, and felt at total peace with all of creation.

After the session, Rosa was filled with such incredible Love and gratitude she went back to her family a completely changed woman. In the few short hours since her arrival, she had reached a place inside where she could truthfully Love herself. For Rosa, freeing her heart was the first step on a new journey, following the path of her soul and receiving all the gifts of Spirit.

Accepting a New Relationship

Another important factor in considering the healing of any issue is honoring the timing of the whole process and not just the session itself. Many unresolved emotional dramas have taken lifetimes to accumulate. Allowing them the time and space to unravel is important.

Madeleine was serious about finding a relationship right for her. In her mid-forties, she hadn't had a primary relationship for years. Divorced with two children, the pain had been too much.

What was appropriate for Madeleine was a series of Heart Awakening sessions over several months. She gradually went through all the past relationships with her family, her first husband, her boss, herself, and her children. Every session was directed to one key relationship or another, until she saw the perfection within each one and her heart felt complete.

The hardest relationship to face was the one with her father. But eventually she experienced his Divine essence, and felt free because she finally understood the source of her fears about men. A few days after that session, Madeleine called, excited about having met someone new, and six months later was married. She found herself involved in a genuine, solid relationship.

She knew the inner work she did on herself made it possible for her to attract a mate of much higher quality than she might otherwise have done. What was of value to her was knowing she didn't have to force the issue and when she was ready, her partner appeared. In a previous session, Madeleine had connected with the essence of her mate-to-be. She wasn't sure who he was, but knew when they connected, she would know. Then she was able to let him go and trust they would meet sooner or later. When the time came, her ability to feel the connection with him was all she needed.

Changing Your Career

Sometimes you might not be ready to accept or experience the shift you have asked for on the day of the Heart Awakening session. Sometimes you need to go through other life experiences before getting the message.

Joyce went to work the day after her Heart Awakening session. She had reached a powerful space inside herself, yet more was needed. When she got to work she couldn't handle being there. Being in the energy of her workplace was necessary for Joyce to realize the contradiction between her spirituality and her work in a law firm handling cases against the environment. She handed in her notice that day. No matter what, truth had to prevail, even if it meant the loss of a very well-paying job.

Seeing Your Career from a New Perspective

Heart Awakening is the capacity to remember the Divine within and have a much greater level of discernment about what is of Godliness and what isn't.

It was three or four years before Cheryl was ready to act on what she had experienced in her Heart Awakening session. Her heart was touched in a profound way, but she had to finish college before she could rearrange her life based upon her discovery. What she found was that the truth of her existence was not just in the world of thought and emotion but was much deeper in the world of energy and love. Everything she learned at college served her, but now she saw life from a different set of priorities. Never again could she really believe that what she was thinking and feeling was real. The value of her session was that it prevented her from going in directions too far removed from a heart-centered approach to life.

Converting Negative Emotions into Love

There is a big difference between simply recreating the pain of the past and releasing the pain. When Spirit is brought into the healing process, the unresolved emotions dissolve, never to be recreated. Chronic emotional problems are reflected in different parts of the body's electromagnetic field. As they are released, a deep sense of unconditional love within is discovered. The experience is so rich and rewarding it is impossible to go back to the old ways.

Heart Awakening isn't just about getting you to emote. Emotions or energies in motion become blocked due to negative beliefs and faulty perception accumulated through the course of life. Their complete release only comes when you are ready to perceive life the way Spirit would have you perceive it.

I like to think of God as the part in us and all creation that is infinitely wise and totally, unconditionally loving. This is always present, wanting to be released and revealed. It has never gone away, nor does it have to be created. When it comes to expressing emotions to convert negative energy into unconditional Love, Heart Awakening sessions provide the training.

In ordinary emotional dumping - kicking pillows or shouting to get physiological relief - there is no management of the energy. It is thrown out with the hope something will be accomplished. Then later we wonder why the same emotional pattern keeps resurfacing. This is the level of the ego hoping to heal itself. For the healing to occur and the shift to be permanent, we need to express unresolved negative emotions in such a way that negativity is converted into unconditional Love without blaming another person or causing them to withdraw. The ego doesn't always know how to do this and can't when it cannot love unconditionally no matter how hard it tries.

It is Spirit within us that expresses Love. The words aren't thought about beforehand; they can't be controlled. When they come from the energy of the present moment, it is no longer the ego speaking but Spirit within speaking. People find themselves expressing ideas in ways they never thought possible. Spirit gives the words that come out, one by one.

When our intention is to restore unconditional love, Spirit gives us a flow of insight to heal our perceptions and show us the inherent divinity within everything. The gateway is through the heart. The more genuine the decision to restore wholeness and Love to relationships with self and others, the more Spirit shows us Love is the only thing real. This is when true healing occurs. When the heart is open and Love is felt, the rest is just the meandering journey the ego takes as it surrenders to the truth of who we are in our Divine essence.

With alignment and preparation, Spirit brings even the simplest words to heal the greatest pain. A corner is lifted off the endless veil of darkness that has shrouded human endeavors, and complete transformation is possible. We are entering a new age - the age of an open heart. Participation in all the good transpiring on earth today begins with unconditionally loving self.

CHAPTER 10

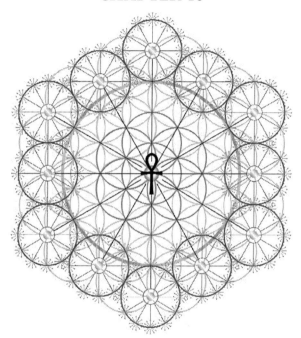

RECONNECTING WITH YOUR
DIVINE MIND

Is your mind separate or unified? A mind that accepts and responds to its moment-to-moment connection with the Divine is a mind that knows peace, love and unity. A mind that believes itself to be an ego separate from the Divine is a mind that believes in fear, doubt and error.

Both minds draw from the same source but with two totally different functions. There is a stage in spiritual self-development when it is no longer appropriate to gather information and knowledge through the intellect in an attempt to fashion God in the ego's image. Rather, the spiritual ambitions of the ego are laid to rest in favor of receiving knowledge of all things directly from the Divine Mind, the infinite reservoir from which all states of creative potential emanate.

The Divine Mind

The Divine Mind has faith in the totality of universal abundance and responds to life with full trust in the inherent perfection within all life. It lives in the present moment with a deep acceptance it is forever a part of the universe. The Divine Mind serves the laws Spirit would extend and share and is in acceptance of One energy and continuously serves to extend that One energy. Having all knowledge of all things, it releases the forces of Divine Love, Divine Power, and Divine Wisdom into a continuous stream of creative expression based on Spirit's perception of the situation at hand.

The Divine Mind is a part of self within that has

forever been in touch with the totality of all truth. When expression seeks to expand this truth, the energy radiates out, triggering the awakening of Divine consciousness and touching all with the memory of their soul's purpose. That alignment reveals a way of life that brings peace and reflects the Divine Will. It ultimately leads to a partnership of the ego and Spirit, and guides and frees the soul.

The Now Moment

The first step to having a direct relationship with the Divine is to learn to relax into the vast emptiness of the present moment. A doorway opens, giving us the ability to see the glorious beauty of the energies contained within Divinity. The "now" moment is a spiraling movement throughout eternity. Linear time exists within the chromosomes and chakras of the body by virtue of our belief in a nonexistent past and future. Within the power contained in the present moment, we can choose to stop over-identifying with the body-mind mechanism and know ourselves as pure consciousness, which is energy. With all the channels of energy in the body open, we reveal our true self and express it.

Pure Consciousness

The next step is to recognize self as pure consciousness. It is who we are and consciousness is energy revealing itself in the now moment. It is the life-force energy returned and realigned for its rightful purpose - to expand and grow in the extending of all that gives life. Truly knowing peace of mind begins when all thoughts, beliefs and feelings are recognized for what they are - the glamour and illusion into which we chose to invest our life-force energy. The moment we recognize there is no truth in the outer mind, we can relax into being pure consciousness. This allows all of the entanglements, past and future, to begin to gently dissolve into what they are - nothing.

Accepting Spirit

Once pure consciousness is attained, it is possible to raise your frequency to the level of energy where Spirit presides. To relax into that level is to discover an entire world of experience beyond the ordinary understanding of the ego. The futility of the outer mind's quest is seen with such clarity you are forever grateful for the ego's inability to succeed. Divine Love is felt so strongly you find the space where you recognize the truth of your own perfection. In the acceptance of the totality of Spirit's perception, the inherent perfection within all life is revealed to you. This is beyond thought, yet all is understood. It is the key that opens the heart and restores the ability to love self fully.

Manifesting the Divine in Your Life

Once we learn to relax into the present moment, become aware of the presence of Spirit and merge our consciousness with the Divine, we can free ourselves of the distorted thinking and manifest a life truly in line with Divine will.

The first step is to open your heart to an inner awareness of the priority you are seeking to manifest in your life today. Relax into that quiet space within and listen for the answer in the heart, not the head. Once determined, keep the thought that came to you in mind and offer it into Spirit's hands for manifestation. For example, you might have a deep desire to experience peace. One part of you holds the thought of "peace" while another focuses on its connection with Spirit, knowing that Spirit has infinite power and ability to bring about any change you desire. Gently repeat the thought "peace" to yourself over and over, all day if necessary and allow the inner state of consciousness to manifest.

This is like communion with the Divine or a form of prayer, if you want to look at it that way. The purpose of repetition is to stabilize the outer mind and allow Spirit to bring the insights and understanding needed to bring peace into whatever situation is at hand. A thought held in connection with the Divine has all the power to materialize, be it the manifesting of a new state of consciousness or a desired objective in the physical reality. If what you are seeking is in the Divine will, the energy is there and manifestation will flow. Eventually the thoughts need no longer be held in the outer mind and are simply replaced with pure intent.

Healing Self

The world is filled with people who want to change their lives for the better. On one level, the growth and transformation of daily living is the way to realize self in our higher expression. On another level, we need to remember who we are is pure consciousness and whatever we are conscious of is but a construct of beliefs, feelings and images that form a part of our personality. What we are conscious of is life and we can enjoy and share in all the gifts it has to offer. But when we become attached to what we are conscious of and want it to be a part of us, it is magnetized toward us; when it comes from fear, distortions in our electrical bodies begin. It is only when we step into knowing who we are - consciousness - and what we are - love - that we connect with the power of Spirit's presence and can change the nature of our reactions to life at will. The entire construction of our personality consists of images, beliefs and feelings lying within our aura, none of which have any greater hold over us than any other.

When we can bring time to a standstill and raise our consciousness to Spirit's level, we can literally change anything and everything going on within. Once a thought or feeling is identified as in need of being released, simply observe it, feel into the energy behind it, and decide what you want to change it into. Then bring in Spirit's assistance to help you create the thought form, feeling or image with which you want it replaced. Remember, it is about surrendering the ways of the ego, not creating ideas to build the ego.

Loving And Accepting Self

Heart Awakening sessions are an introduction to the levels of energy and inner experiences where all of this can occur. Ultimately, there is but one idea we are to accept in its totality. This is to fully love and accept ourselves just the way God intended. Accomplishing this without the Grace of Spirit can be a long, drawn out, day-by-day challenge. However, the depth and qualities of energy available during a Heart Awakening session make this incredible experience a reality for anyone who is sincere.

Freeing Yourself from Discarnate Entities

Some people are drawn to a session because they have experienced an event in their lives that caused a major depletion of their life-force energy. Such an event might have been a long and serious illness or a trauma like a car accident. It might be the removal of an organ or gland, such as ovaries or gall bladder. Others whose energies are low are involved with drugs and alcohol, and then there are those who can't break loose from an intense pattern of negativity. Even when they have experienced many different healing modalities, they still find themselves in an emotional pit from which they cannot escape.

The problem sometimes lies in one or several discarnate entities attaching themselves to an organ, gland, or part of the electromagnetic field. Such an attachment can be caused by any number of events, most of which deal with the depletion of life-force energy. These entities have the effect of draining energy from the part of the body to which they are attached. With the presence of Spirit, these can be freed from a person's aura.

If the attachment is coupled with damage to the electromagnetic field, it is harder to get free from these influences. The more damage to the aura, the more susceptible we are to having attachments anchored in the physical body. When the chakras are damaged, there may be an attachment to the corresponding gland or organ.

A discarnate entity is also known as astral consciousness and closely relates to the emotional body. It is an energetic imprint of the day-to-day thoughts and feelings it accumulated while on earth. When you incarnated, only a portion of your soul descended into the earth realm; the majority of it stayed in the heaven worlds. The portion with you on earth returns to the heaven worlds upon physical death. The astral consciousness moves to the astral plane where it continues its journey until the astral shell is dropped, much in the same way the physical body is dropped, and it completes what wasn't learned during its incarnation.

Completing lessons on the astral planes is much more difficult than doing it in the physical body because everything is much more vivid. Fears seem more real, making them more difficult to release. Not having a physical body to reflect what is going on makes it harder to let go. That is why it is so important to learn to love self unconditionally and complete our lessons while on the earth plane.

After a violent physical death or death involving a strong attachment to something in the material world, an astral consciousness can become a problem for a person on earth. The most common attachments are drugs, alcohol, a person, or even a material possession. The deceased astral consciousness stays bound to the earth plane and tries to satisfy its needs by attaching itself to someone with a similar pattern. An example is someone who left the body (physical death) because of alcohol abuse. The astral consciousness, without the indwelling Spirit, finds another earth-bound person who drinks heavily. Perceiving this individual to be a light, the astral consciousness attaches itself and gradually seeks to satisfy its craving for alcohol through the unwary drinker. The drinker gets drunk one night, never really feels right again, and continues to deepen his drinking habit, feeding himself and the discarnate who also wants a drink. It becomes harder and harder for the drinker to break the habit. A downward spiral continues, often until the situation becomes life-threatening.

The discarnate astral consciousness can be a challenge to someone coming for a Heart Awakening session because, facing eviction, it may try to sabotage a healing attempt. More often than not, people arrive at a session after they have given up the drugs or alcohol yet still seriously need assistance.

It is valuable to remember that a lower astral consciousness doesn't have Spirit within and is actually harmless. Often trapped in a negative, narrow frame of thought, it doesn't have the capacity to do much. An astral consciousness can be guided back to its soul once it is ready to let go.

This is approached in a Heart Awakening by unraveling and releasing the core negative emotion. Because of the prayers, the assistance of the angelic realm, and the high energies pouring in to repair the electromagnetic field, it is possible for a person to be freed from these astral influences.

Other areas where entities can be a problem are highly charged, negative emotional states like a severe quarrel between two people. A person with a strong electromagnetic energy field may not have a permanent attachment lodged into the body, but could still be susceptible to influence from the astral plane. Quarrels can be particularly intense because they are a breeding ground for lower astral influences.

Any unusually negative and constant situation creates susceptibility and may well be a reason for having a Heart Awakening. During the session, a tremendous amount of light and energy is poured in and the entities can't stand it and leave.

The frequency of clear light and the presence of Spirit prevent an astral consciousness from influencing someone. With appropriate prayers, an astral influence can be released back to its soul. It is important to repair the damaged aura and clear the underlying emotional pattern to prevent another attachment. Sometimes a program of self-maintenance is needed to anchor in the light.

Astral influences are surprisingly common in chronic emotional and physical problems. The full bodily possession by an astral consciousness is much less frequent. As the earth prepares us, it seems to be easier and easier to release them. They are nothing to fear. They don't belong here and simply need to be told in no uncertain terms they must leave. With faith and Divine intervention, they can be freed to continue their journey back to their soul.

Freeing Yourself
from Elemental Thought Forms

It is important to differentiate between an elemental thought form and a discarnate entity. The latter we have discussed. The former is actually more serious. An astral consciousness can be dispelled and released with relative ease by someone who knows how. However, the real problems in people's auras are elemental thought entities.

Each time we create a thought form and believe it to be true, the elements of earth, air, water, and fire blend together to give that thought a material substance. This is called an elemental thought form. When we energize a positive or negative thought pattern, we give life to those thoughts. The increased accumulation of elemental thought forms attracts more thoughts of a like nature, building a web we know as our personality.

Quite often, in any close relationship, it is possible to create a whole web of positive and negative thought forms about self or another person. Any thought about self that the ego is identified with readily projects onto another. As we build a picture of what we think another person is like, we construct a web of elemental thought forms about them within our own auric field, not realizing thoughts never leave their place of origin, namely self.

The real gift of Heart Awakening is about learning not to judge self or others. This is very important, because this can create strong elemental thought forms that we keep. Strongly energized positive or negative elemental thought forms can grow to discolor and distort the electrical bodies, making it difficult for Divine energy to flow smoothly through the aura. Some of these elemental thought forms can grow to several feet in length. Over a period of many years, all kinds of emotional, mental, physical and spiritual problems can build up. For example, we may not perceive another person as they really are, but continually respond to our projected idea of who we think they are.

Elemental thought forms need to be dissolved through forgiveness, Love, the help of Spirit, and taking responsibility for perceiving life the way Spirit would have us perceive it. Heart Awakening sessions are designed to help dissolve the distortions of elemental thought forms so they never return. It is somewhat like deflating a balloon filled with suppressed emotions and is extremely freeing.

A person working on the elimination of elemental thought forms may need a period of adjustment. Part of the follow-up with Heart Awakening is learning to draw in the universal energy from Spirit to replace what has been dissolved. Regular prayer, meditation, and spiritual study become an essential part of the return to wholeness.

Repairing Your Aura

How do you know when there is damage to the electromagnetic field? Any chronic physical disorder, psychological "gap," or break in consciousness indicates a damaged energy field. Whenever you find yourself engaging in an activity and you can't handle it or hit an emotional wobbly, it's a sign of possible damage to the electrical bodies in the aura. It is the same with a pattern of physical pain, which is a function of the energy channels not flowing properly.

No damage is permanent because the fifth layer of the aura contains the blueprint of the perfected Self. Some situations can be corrected easily; others take time. A great gift comes from healing the aura because patterns that seemed impossible to heal can completely disappear, never to return. Sometimes the outer self feels uncomfortable with the work being done to the aura, but the inner self is always happy because, when healing is approached this way, there is a completion and freeing of the soul. The knowing that comes from this type of healing releases a whole new level of energy and creative expression.

Sometimes people are drawn to sessions because of excessive leaks and damage to their electromagnetic field. Typically, most of us have a number of areas around which the energy has become blocked. These blockages often represent our life's work in terms of the inner growth we need, but sometimes the aura is so damaged we become hypersensitive to anything going on around us. This damage can manifest in many ways. One might experience difficulty being around people, an inability to cope within high-stress work environments, or a person may have tried to balance a particular part of his or her body without success. If nothing seems to be effective, a damaged or leaking aura may be the cause.

These situations often require work over a period of time with training on how to manage life-force energy. Until damaged chakras or leaks are repaired, life can be very challenging.

Molly suffered with severe digestive problems most of her life. A Heart Awakening session revealed a need for a series of sessions to repair the damage to her solar plexus chakra, which governs the ability to do things in life. An accumulation of unresolved fears had created the damage. The day-to-day business of life made it impossible for her to relax enough to let the wound settle, so it was continually re-aggravated.

The healing work helped her release most of the fears about herself. As the leaks were repaired over a period of time, Molly found herself more capable of handling her life. Her courage and natural zest for living returned and she learned simple QiGong exercises to practice daily. When she learned to harness the universal life-force energy for herself, she found it was the key to her health, joy, and abundance. The more she developed her spirituality, the easier it became to attract material abundance.

The enthusiasm Molly built from regenerating herself in the energy allowed her to experience more of life. All she needed to keep herself in balance was to relax and spend a couple of hours each day enjoying herself, not focusing on anything particular, just allowing herself to open up to the vastness of empty space. The more she did this, the more real energy she experienced.

The energy filtered through all her beingness, and gradually her physical aches and pains melted away and Molly released her attachment to focusing on them. After a while, she recognized what a gift her damaged electromagnetic field had been. It had incapacitated her to the point where she had to let go of thinking and worrying. She learned energy

follows thought and she had directed so much negative ener-
gy toward herself that she literally had to stop thinking to
heal herself.

As the life-force energy regenerated her body, Molly dis-
covered deep Love on a permanent, day-by-day basis. The
more she basked in the energy, the more she could observe the
natural flow of events unfolding themselves before her.
Molly was no longer in charge on an ego level, allowing
events to take their natural course and follow the flow to
where the energy was directing her. By her continued habit
of emptying herself each day and finding her connection
with the universal energy, Molly discerned which aspects of
her life she should focus on and which were better left alone.

What had been an unacceptable sensitivity to the nega-
tivity around her turned into a heightened awareness of the
impulses of Spirit. The more Molly relaxed, emptied her
mind, and let go, the clearer her inner guidance became.
She found she didn't need to think of problems as much
because solutions presented themselves before she could formu-
late the problem with her outer mind. The brain was con-
tinually releasing everything - shifting, emptying - and
when something was needed, the answer would be there. At
a fundamental level, her Heart Awakening session helped
Molly dive deeply enough into her own essence to experience
the truth of who she really was. She found truth lay
beyond the outer mind, and she released the outer identifica-
tion with her ego.

Energy Following Thought

Another powerful aspect of Heart Awakening sessions is the in-depth understanding and healing of
the chakras and layers of the aura. The source of

every physical pain lies in a congestion of thought patterns represented as energy blockages in the aura. Part of the Heart Awakener's training deals with learning to recognize the issues and where they reside in the aura. When these blockages are cleared, the gifts of spiritual awareness are available at a much higher level and lead to a profound communion with the Divine.

One important aspect of moving from conventional therapy to a spiritual approach to healing is releasing the need to label particular conditions. Energy follows thought and labeling creates negative conditions, like identification with what is being labeled rather than the wholeness that already exists. Releasing labels allows your natural wholeness to be revealed. Not naming a condition brings energy without limitations.

Our souls naturally bring us to all the life experiences we need, and how we respond to them creates our personality. The thought forms assigned to an event are what give it reality. The idea behind Heart Awakening is to dissolve negative thought forms. Our negative perception of the way something happened cannot recur after a Heart Awakening. Certainly, the soul retains a memory of the experience for its growth and understanding, but our emotional reaction has been dissolved.

This is where the true challenge of the healing process occurs: to focus continually on the reality that is an expression of our wholeness instead of being trapped by patterns of the past. The accumulated energetic effects of past patterning are dissolved during sessions. The more this is done, the more we release the whole being we know ourselves to be into full manifestation. By dissolving who we are not, we allow our true Self to be present in our day-to-day lives.

CHAPTER 11

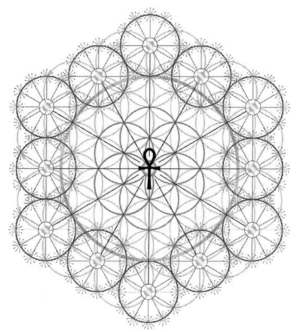

FOCUSING ON YOUR SPIRITUAL
GROWTH

Heart Awakening serves as a catalyst to help you reach a new level in your spiritual growth, regardless of spiritual beliefs or religious background. The Heart Awakening experience can be integrated into any religion or spiritual path you have chosen to follow. Heart Awakening's purpose is to guide us to the tangible experience of Divine Love that is the common goal of all spiritual paths. Each session stands alone. Yet over time, the process can be used for different types of spiritual experiences that may be necessary on your path. Some may be chosen, some unexpected, but each offers you major revelations to set you free in a way you never dreamed possible.

During Heart Awakening, the combination of prayer, energy work and perceiving everything through the heart opens up your unlimited spiritual potential. If the genuineness of the heart is there and the moment is appropriate, Spirit always responds. Sometimes the results may seem too much for the ego to integrate, but when Spirit gifts you with certain thought forms, they inevitably work themselves through into your daily life.

Rediscovering God

One of the major hurdles to rediscovering God is the ego personality creating God in its own image. No matter how hard the ego personality self tries to extend love and intimacy to this illusory image, it cannot respond. This is why Heart Awakening is so important to spiritual growth. It opens the heart in such a way we can truly re-establish direct contact with our Divine Self to fulfill the most profound desires for unconditional love and joy. Once you are genuinely ready and willing to let go of the ego's illusions, nothing can stand in the way of your reunion with the ultimate love of your life.

Mary came to me for a Heart Awakening session. For so long, she had craved the feeling of Divine Love in her heart. She thought of God as an authority figure outside of herself to whom she turned for answers. She couldn't experience the God within as a purely non-judgmental, totally unconditionally loving presence who fully supported her on all levels of life's journey.

Hardly had the opening prayer of the session begun when Spirit gently washed out a mountain of pain and sorrow. Mary could feel Spirit's presence in the room, knew her prayers were being answered, and knew angelic beings were present. Within a short time, her heart was filled with a glorious memory of herself centered in the light. She was ready for her spiritual essence to shine forth once again. The true breakthrough came when Mary finally forgave herself for the guilt she felt for her perceived failure to connect deeply with God throughout her life. Through the session she released more and more of the anger and frustration she had unconsciously directed towards God because of her feelings of separation from her Divine Self. Once able to emotionally and physiologically experience the intense flood of pure unconditional love from God, all of Mary's misery and anger dissolved.

Gaining Self-Control

Heart Awakening sessions can also bring you to a specific experience of a higher level of spiritual awareness.

Jim wanted to free himself of excessive control issues with women. During his Heart Awakening session, he was led through an intense series of profound inner revelations about himself. As a result, he experienced a state beyond all thought where true inner peace reigned. Jim had complete self-control in this state and no longer needed to control others or be controlled by them.

This was the missing piece he had been seeking. Jim realized Divine self-control is actually effortless, and bestows the power of ultimate control on all creation because no control of anything is required in the world of Spirit. He released the need to think and control life through the ego and surrendered into the vastness of space in the present moment. Within this moment, Jim experienced the distinction between the will of the outer self and the Divine Will which moves unquestionably through the material world - not controlling, but manifesting and implementing God's great plan for all creation. Perfect self-control would allow the natural abundance of the universe to flow his way.

Reclaiming Spiritual Gifts

Laura had prayed for a long time to find her own deep inner experience of the Divine. During her second Heart Awakening session, Laura remembered she had well-developed intuitive and psychic abilities as a child. She had misused these abilities to manipulate those around her, particularly her mother. Laura found she could get her needs met by sending out intense psychic energy prompting her mother to do things for her. The result was a rift with her mother.

It also led to a major difficulty within Laura about her

feminine energy. She had developed lumps in her breast and suffered a complete loss of her spiritual gifts.

As these deep patterns were released, Laura experienced herself as pure light. Bathed in its vastness, she felt a massive influx of energies pouring through every cell of her body. She felt herself being purified as if on fire from head to toe.

Laura had finally unraveled why she had so many fears about using her spiritual gifts. Her session reconnected her to Divine Love, allowing her to reclaim the use of her spiritual abilities. The lumps in her breast disappeared.

Laura had used her Heart Awakening session to accelerate her spiritual growth to a much higher level of experience. She needed the experience to get past an intellectual understanding of her spirituality.

Expanding Your Capacity to Love

Although many people come to sessions because they are in a challenging personal situation, sessions are also a vehicle to bring you to the next level of your spiritual growth. Heart Awakening was developed to help people have a deep mystical experience of the Divine.

This isn't necessarily the focus of every session, but when I first opened my heart to the true spiritual essence of who I am, I knew humanity's ability to move forward is limited only by its capacity to know God within. It became my life's work to help others experience this state and restore their full faith in the inherent Divinity within themselves and all life. Faith in the Divine is what we remember from a session long after the details and insights that brought the experience have passed.

155

Gerry was already wide open and beaming in his heart when he came in. Still, he wanted to deepen his understanding of his spirituality. His Heart Awakening session proved more difficult than he anticipated. The limitless capacity and breadth of Divine Love overwhelmed him. As he released layer upon layer of ego limitation, his energy field grew with an incredible golden color that filled the entire room. The presence of the angels engulfed him. He had gone into the session intending to expand his ability to bathe in the Love and his desire was well rewarded. His energy field glowed with new, vibrant colors, and he allowed it to expand as far as his mind could reach.

Gerry felt linked to everything and everyone on earth. He perceived lines of energy running to infinity in every direction, scintillating with an active intelligence in the light itself. He felt the awesome consciousness of the Divine extending itself through all people and all things and was completely mesmerized by the intricacies of pattern and shape in the light. He felt the very fabric of existence and the wisdom and Love within the vastness of the energy awed him.

It was like shifting into a new dimension of reality. Gerry felt the desire and intention of the energy in its unconditionalness - always waiting to be brought forward, always smiling, always knowing, never doubting, and in complete understanding. He realized this energy contained such immaculate creative power it knew everything. It was the Source which bound his body together. He experienced himself as pure energy, with the physical body attached as an appendage, a denser part. His real Self was pure energy, everlasting and eternal. It was a space in which he felt he could stay forever. It was a place where he knew himself as himself.

Gerry learned the depth of the link between energy and thought and in that space, could direct loving thoughts to his family. He could feel the beam of energy going to them across time and space. He knew his mind was powerful, but never realized how powerful it was when linked with this one energy. He discovered the place where God's will and free will become one and it was the goal his soul was seeking.

Gerry reached such a level of deep resolution within himself in one session he was able to go into the full-time healing work he desired. The experience brought him into a deep communion with Spirit where he knew what he could offer to others was genuine. He now knew the purpose of all healing was to reconnect us to the Divine Love. When he left, he was grateful, awakened, driven, and empowered as he had never been before.

Connecting with Spiritual Teachers

During a Heart Awakening session, many people are able to connect with the angelic realm, their guides or teachers on the inner planes. Some people are able to make contact for the first time and receive the names of their guides and teachers. You might discover the more you get into your heart, the easier it is to see and hear them. From them, you accept insights into situations in your life for which you need answers. Once the ice is broken, you gain the ability to maintain daily contact.

Annabel had a very interesting session. She was taken back to a time just before she was born. With her guides and teachers, she saw the purpose for her incarnation on earth and discovered her primary lesson was to be an independent self-reliant individual. Simply accepting this as her lesson made a major shift possible because she had been resisting the need for independence all her life.

In addition, contacting her guides was special. It helped Annabel remember the commitment she and her guides had made to fulfill this lesson on earth. She felt their Love for her and the appreciation they had for her challenging life path. Annabel realized her guides could help her with anything she needed and that made her feel more peaceful and confident. She wasn't alone and never had been. Straying from her ability to connect with Divine Love had made her feel disconnected from her guides.

More importantly, Annabel realized her guides weren't there to do everything for her. She often prayed to them to get things done. By talking to them during her session, she realized how much they were there simply to provide guidance and support when she needed it. Her heart melted as she felt their love and compassion, and the complete absence of judgment they had for her learning process.

Annabel had been a victim of abuse as a child, and the concept of unconditional Love was difficult for her to accept. But as her guides spoke to her, she was reassured because it felt safe to have support she could trust. This knowledge gave her strength and courage. It allowed her to feel valued for who she was and not for the pain she carried. In her heart she accepted what she needed to do and it set her free.

Spiritual Wisdom Coming to Life

Solutions from Spirit leave no questions. They are complete, free of any trace of the ego, and solve the problems at hand. They empower you to become all you came to earth to be and the solutions never hurt anyone. They are simply a statement, an acceptance of what is. They leave the heart open and give life. There is always such grace and power in these Divine solutions you are given a real sense of purpose and direction. They remove doubt and release a flow of abundance that reminds you of your eternal connection with the Divine. Spirit's job is not to have you change the outer world, but to change your perception of the world so you see it through the eyes of love and compassion. All outer changes stem from knowing and following Spirit's purpose for any given situation. Heart Awakening brings spiritual wisdom to life.

Fred flew in from England for a seven-day Heart Awakening retreat. A corporate executive, he had an intellectual understanding of spirituality. But although Fred felt intellectually prepared for a Heart awakening session, his session surprised him.

At first, Fred was afraid of the Divine energies flowing through every cell of his physical body, but soon realized Heart Awakening was bringing him a tangible experience of the essence flowing through all life. The congestion of thought forms created by the personality had inhibited the flow of this energy, and no amount of intellectual work had been able to substitute for the direct experience of true Divine Wisdom. Fred was reminded of the Kabbalah, which teaches all the branches of the Tree of Life flow through the heart. Once he experienced his heart being opened, all its virtues came to life and were no longer just an intellectual understanding. He experienced them as real qualities alive and active within him.

Fred connected with his guides and teachers. Divine Love was no longer something his ego was aimlessly searching for - it was a living, breathing, dynamic energy filling every cell and fiber of his being. It brought him back to the memory of his Divine essence.

Fred gave all of himself during that week and received a vision showing him his days in the corporate world were over. He was to become a living representation of the Divine essence and carry the energy far and wide to help others awaken to their truth of who they are.

Loving from Within

The greatest gift of a session quite often is ending the ego's futile search for love. Typically, the last line of defense for the ego is trying to find love from an outside relationship. Love lies within and grows in the experience of itself only when given from a place of knowing its unlimited nature. Many spiritual ambitions have been changed when Spirit brings the understanding necessary to help people release the need to search for love outside of themselves.

Roger set high goals for what he wanted to accomplish spiritually and studied extensively to improve his spiritual understanding. But during his Heart Awakening session, he realized, despite all of his learning, it was actually his ego demanding enlightenment.

To evolve spiritually, Roger needed to be of service by healing and teaching and then, through him, Spirit could do the real work of transmitting Divine energies. When Roger realized he couldn't know God without serving God, his spiritual ambition was laid to rest.

The Principle of Acceptance

Lori's session was another example of how spiritual wisdom comes to life. Lori had a long history of difficulties with

*her father image. Her father abused her as a child, her mar-
riage was very challenging, and she was having trouble rec-
onciling her relationship with an earlier spiritual teacher
who was also male. In spite of many years living in a spiritual community, she was having difficulty finding God.*

*Her session exemplified the principle of the need for accep-
tance of her own Divinity. During her Heart Awakening,
Lori reached a place inside herself where she realized she
had never been taught to accept herself as a Divine being.
Lori had spent many years struggling to find peace and
only when she accepted that peace was hers by choice was its
experience open to her.*

*Once she accepted who she really was, she saw her rela-
tionship to the Father God in a new light - full of unconditional Love and Wisdom. Her revelation opened her heart
and her resentment and hatred of men melted away. By
experiencing and seeing her Divine Self during her session,
she was able to whole-heartedly accept her own true divinity
and open up to God's gifts and presence within her.*

Serving Spirit

*Peter had a long history of self-improvement workshops
behind him and each offered temporary inspiration, but
nothing of lasting value. During a weeklong Heart
Awakening workshop in Hawaii, he avoided having a session until the very last day when he felt he was about to go
home disappointed.*

*During Peter's session, the energy work built a beautiful,
sharp shield of energy all around him. I looked out and
saw the glistening sun with dolphins swimming in the
background. It was a paradise setting. I looked into the
depth of Peter's soul to feel what would set him free. In the*

energy, and through the grace of Spirit, all Peter needed to hear were the words, "It's time for you to be of service."

In that moment, those words and the way they were said were all Peter needed. He burst into tears, feeling Spirit carry him through a sense of revelation that left his heart with no uncertainty. He knew the solution to his pain was to fully commit to a life of service to the Divine, following its guidance rather than his ego's agenda. He knew in his heart it was right. He had feared it for so long because he knew his ego would rebel. It didn't want to have to go through the daily task of surrendering to the expression of his true Self. For him to make the shift, Peter needed to experience raw Divine power flooding through his whole being. He couldn't have known where to go spiritually without a taste of the Divine. Spirit had spoken; the rest was up to him.

While Peter's session was going on, Bill, a veteran Qi-Gong master, was assisting Peter's Heart Awakening. Bill understood the Chi (or life-force) energy well, having dedicated most of his life to it. But what he witnessed at the table with Peter astounded him because he had never seen how energy could be used to open the heart. He observed how the Chinese were masters at healing with energy, but never understood how it could dissolve suppressed emotion and open the heart in such a powerful way. Bill felt the impact of Spirit's energy and it was all he needed to open his heart in a new and powerfully profound way. He felt the raw strength of Spirit's energy envelop him and offer him the gift of healing his own heart. The Heart Awakening energy, omniscient and omnipresent, was the same, but the healings experienced by these two men were different and entirely appropriate for each of them.

PART D
WHY DOES HEART
AWAKENING WORK?

CHAPTER 12

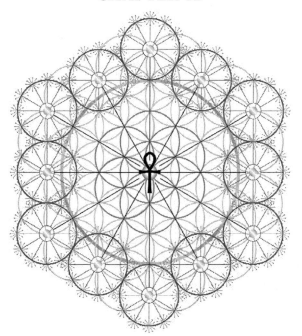

FINDING YOUR DIVINE
WITHIN

Heart Awakening is a powerful and effective means of discovering and deepening the Divine Love within. One of the main reasons is because the healing sessions allow for a formless, creative, moment-to-moment expression that opens the way for the gifts of Spirit to do their work.

As the underlying intent of each session is always to fulfill our desire to commune with the Divine, the sessions teach us the ways we can develop a lifestyle dedicated to living in the heart. They also teach us the difference between the Divine and the ego so that we can learn how to recognize genuine purity of heart.

Through Spirit, the unmistakable magical presence of Divine Love reveals itself and you remember this energy because it is so familiar to you. It is a high, refined frequency that brings peace and the gift of discernment where we can recognize truth and genuine purity of heart.

Purity of intention and desire open the doorway for anyone to enjoy a full healing. Spirit is omniscient and works through all types of personal background without presupposing need or placing obligations on giver or receiver. Spirit honors purity of intention and a genuine desire to explore the miracles of heart-centered awareness.

Heart Awakening sessions are pure simplicity. They bring Love forward through gentle reminders of what is already known but not being accepted and acted upon. Sessions revolve around trusting in Divine perfection. When the need for a session is present, the soul's desire is present. The timing is right in the present moment and God's hand becomes known. All else reveals itself within the flow. The release and the shift occur in your consciousness because it is time to accept what in God's world must naturally be and release what is not.

Heart Awakening sessions challenge you to delve further into yourself to find the answers you have been seeking. Once you experience the depth to which they can take you, a whole new vista opens up on life. You can allow who you really are to be revealed to yourself and to the world.

Reclaiming Your Wholeness

Heart Awakening is an answer to our prayers when we long to return to our hearts but are unable to find the way alone. Sessions work because people are ready and want them to work. The Awakener simply holds the knowing that the person on the table is whole and healed and the heart space is ready to be revealed.

Divine consciousness pours into the layers of the auric field and all that is unlike Love has an opportunity to complete itself. The suppressed parts causing the greatest energy blocks and leakages reveal themselves and Divine energies clean and clear the entire luminous egg cocoon of the aura. Spirit leaves nothing out when an electromagnetic field is addressed. It knows its way through all the cracks and crevices, however complex the tangles might be.

Typically, most of us have a number of primary areas where the congestion of thought patterns has coagulated into a mass of energy with which we struggle daily. Through the energy work during Heart Awakening, they can be cleared. We gain the shift in understanding necessary for us to take a huge step forward. Emotional release isn't the purpose of a session, though it frequently is a natural component. Heart Awakening is a breakthrough resulting in a shift of perception that allows Spirit's presence and vibration to bring completion and resolution. Every session helps heal our relationship with the Divine by bringing in the Divine energy and perception.

Heart Awakening differs from counseling or hypnotherapy because the motives for a session concern the ego's surrender rather than its reprogramming. Heart Awakening doesn't try to tell you the way to be, what to do, or try to place a new layer on top of the old. It releases the old and allows Spirit's essence to reveal itself through you. It recognizes that you already know what to do, and simply supports you in living that wholeness. The ego's task is to limit self. Heart Awakening supports your expansion into the unlimited.

A Heart Awakening session reveals your wholeness and helps you let go of feelings trapped by the past. This approach to healing supports you in being all you can be and helps shift your consciousness from identification with the personality into merging with soul and Divine consciousness. This dissolves the elemental thought forms of the past and helps you shift from an ego plagued with unsolvable problems into a true Spirit being. The shift of identity from ego to soul consciousness may take time for you to integrate because it opens up a new way of being. It becomes a moment-by-moment, day-by-day practice, and each step releases more Divine energies into your daily life.

Blending Key Healing Principles

Perhaps the most valuable aspect of a Heart Awakening session is the blending of key healing principles into a single, integrated healing process. Heart Awakening is the result of combining many concepts of heart-centered, spiritual living into an expression that is best for both giver and receiver.

The first principle is development of intuition. Not having the ego to rely on, a Heart Awakener relies on intuition, which frees the person receiving the session to gain insight on a deeper level. To be truly effective, perfect truth must come from Spirit in the moment and not rely on a structured method of healing or the written word.

A session also involves Divine energy in the healing process. The true nature of this energy flow is beyond intellectual understanding, so the practitioner relies on his or her relationship and experience of Divine energies as they unfold within each present moment. The ability to give Heart Awakening sessions involves the cultivation and development of a deep personal relationship with Divine energies. Many people who come to Heart Awakening have extensive experience in the healing arts. Their training provides them with a valuable level of knowledge which serves as a stepping-stone to rely more on their intuition and energy to bring higher levels of soul healing.

Heart Awakening is a unique blend of working with both energy and voice. The voice of the Heart Awakener during a session takes on a unique style and quality filled with love and compassion. It is an extension and expression of the Divine.

Combining energy work with the unique style of a Heart Awakening breakthrough brings about a deeper level of healing. The blend of voice and energy work, coupled with reliance on intuition, is one reason Heart Awakening sessions are so effective.

Focusing on the Divine

Focusing on healing our relationship with the Divine adds further power to Heart Awakening sessions. This addresses the deepest hunger in our souls for full completion of life's challenging issues. When we have learned all Spirit has to teach within a situation, it is done, never to return.

The Heart Awakening process relies on universal spiritual principles true for everyone in all circumstances. It emphasizes the simplicity and depth of the application of these principles rather than the complexities the ego can create.

Another facet of the Heart Awakening blend is the intent of every session to open the heart. God is Love, the Love is within, and true healing involves a return to the Love. The purpose of Heart Awakening is to dissolve everything standing in the way of total love and acceptance of your Self just as you are.

Heart Awakening serves as a bridge between therapy and spiritual realization. On a true spiritual healing level, we are already whole and healed; but on a personality level, most of us feel we have many issues to resolve and clear away. Heart Awakening dissolves the illusion of who we are not by revealing who we are in our Divine perfection.

Finding the Divine in Your Relationships

One of the most powerful aspects of Heart Awakening as an effective healing tool lies in the alignment and purpose of the session - to experience Divine Love between yourself and those with whom you come into contact throughout your life. The underlying intent is always the "Divine within me" experiencing the "Divine within you," and going through the layers of whatever needs resolving until you experience the Divine energetically throughout your body. Once you align this intent with a pure heart, the entire universe - from the Holy Spirit, to the angels, to the God force within - moves in support of this intent and direction. This alignment follows our deepest desires for what we know we must do and yet avoid the most. Our fear of being all we can be inhibits the flow because the personality must surrender completely. Only then will Spirit teach us how to turn negative emotion into unconditional love.

Once we step into the flow of allowing the "Divine within me" to experience the "Divine within you," the Divine presence (Holy Spirit) within takes over. The session unfolds naturally because the deeper self takes over, and the ego is released from its need to analyze and slow down what is going on. There can be no victims, no blame, no withdrawal, no procrastination, no deferring of responsibility, no faulty perception, and no judgment. No part allows incompleteness. By experiencing and honoring the "Divine within me" reaching out to the "Divine within you," everything needed to see the divinity in all your relationships is realized.

Only within this flow can separation between two beings end, separation from God end, and your soul be re-discovered. When you express and resolve, knowing Divine awareness is attentive to everything you say, you receive the gift of an open heart. When you express yourself, knowing God is part of everything being said and done, then Spirit adds blessings and energy, allowing its presence to be felt through you to all others.

Working with Spirit

It is Spirit's job to shift our perceptions and restore our awareness of the inherent Divinity within all things and to reawaken us to experience the Divine Self within. Without it, no true healing can occur.

When I go into the breakthrough portion of a Heart Awakening session, I observe Spirit as a massive, living field of energy lying throughout all levels of a person's being. It is infinite in grace, love, and wisdom. As the breakthrough portion begins, Spirit reveals itself, helping you to unravel the truth of what you need to learn and to feel its presence when you accept your healing.

Spirit is infinite energy and so vast and strong everything changes in its presence. It is incredibly wise and compassionate, capable of entering all the defenses the outer mind can construct.

Spirit carries a knowing that all can and must be healed and extends an offer of that. To experience its presence, your intent must be on restoring your relation with Divine Love. When you accept, you will once again perceive yourself as Divine and move toward the infinite Love of God within yourself and others. Spirit will never cause you pain; but rather invites you to feel complete joy and divine wholeness. The more you are willing to accept your wholeness, the more its energy comes through, correcting all of your perceptions.

During Heart Awakening, Spirit helps you express what is necessary to unravel any portion of your consciousness that is suppressing the Divine, and acknowledges the thought patterns that kept you from knowing its presence. Turning to Spirit and saying, "Show me the way you would have me see this," opens you up to its magic. The most genuine level of truth you can imagine occurs.

The next step is understanding Spirit's power and Love. This understanding fills every particle of your being if you are willing to say what needs expressing to bring Love and resolution to any situation. When the ego lets go, Spirit speaks through you, giving you the words your ego couldn't find. It re-orchestrates your sorrow and turns it into Love because you have been willing to invite Spirit's experience into you. Spirit wants you to ask it to reveal itself to you and help you by letting you know how completely you are loved.

Another observation is the vastness of energy in comparison to the smallness the ego can comprehend.

In some ways, Spirit is like a giant nurturing a tiny lotus blossom and loving it until it loves itself. Its magical touch can heal the words held unexpressed in the emotional body for many lifetimes, dissolving pain. Spirit makes a healing permanent, returning you to the life you have always sought.

To experience Spirit's hand is not difficult. In a Heart Awakening session, Spirit simply asks for an alignment with the energy. The rest is done because you desire it so much that, given the opportunity, you naturally accept what Spirit offers. As you invite its all-loving presence, Spirit will instantly infuse your physical body with its energy and take you one step closer to finding the fullness of your own Divinity within.

CHAPTER 13

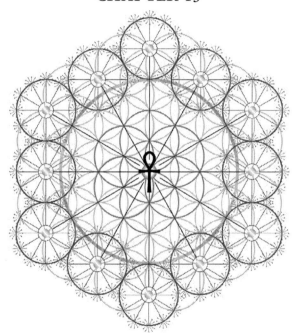

THE POTENTIAL OF HEART
AWAKENING

The potential of what can be done in a Heart Awakening session is limited only by the intensity of the person's desire to free the soul. The true Self can never die, and a single session can bring you back into a full experience of the Divine. This is why Heart Awakening heals. It provides the opportunity to re-inspire yourself to become all you really are in the Divine sense. The greater your desire to reunite with your divinity, the more complete your Heart Awakening will be.

Inner Guidance Through Your Heart

True inner guidance always comes through an open heart. When you experience what it is to per-ceive life through the energies of the heart, freed from an ego that perceives only imperfection, all the inner guidance that is an intrinsic part of our Divine nature will appear.

Once the heart is freed and true inner guidance is revealed, different situations and opportunities open up. Often new connections, new ideas, new possibili-ties come to mind, and life generally flows more easi-ly. In some cases it takes several months for all the benefits of a session to reveal themselves in a person's life. During this time, a continuous and gentle read-justment helps you align your life with your soul's journey. The first and most important step for any-one on the spiritual path is to clear the issues around the heart so true inner guidance can be discerned.

Rich flew in from Kansas for a Heart Awakening session, apprehensive but ready. His life had turned chaotic. An employee had embezzled money from his company the previous year and he had lost his wife in a car accident. He was angry, lonely, confused and had no idea where to go or what to do with his life.

During his session, Rich remembered that as a youngster, he had jettisoned what he valued the most: his capacity to speak from the heart in a clear, honest manner. One day he became angry with his mother and "on a whim" decided not to show his love for her or any other woman ever again. The memory explained why he was withdrawn and unable to release anger or to love his wife during their marriage. He saw how he hadn't taken the time to enjoy his wife and many times went to work when it wasn't necessary. His wife was diagnosed with cancer before the accident and, by seeing the situation through the heart, he now understood why she hadn't wanted to stay on earth.

The session also revealed that Rich's anger was the cumulative effect of not having lived in his heart, making decisions from fear. The decisions created outcomes he didn't like and the anger continued to build. His heart felt he wasn't always making the best choices, and the session showed him what he had done to himself. In part, that was a gift for him so he could learn to grow strong within himself.

Rich now realized he was responsible for much that had gone on with his employee. He had a chance to stop the possibility of embezzlement on a number of occasions but never did anything about it. Instead, he suspected the employee's integrity and allowed his suspicions to color his attitude toward her. Eventually, the situation became impossible for her and she reacted by trying to hurt him through theft. Rich recognized he actually felt guilty about having earned the money in the first place, resulting in his fear attracting the loss of the

177

money. He saw all this through an open heart and was able to forgive himself and his former employee. As a result, he was given the confidence to continue his work.

The session was extremely powerful and released Rich's fear of being alone, poor, and unloved. He regained his sense of self-worth by coming to grips with what his heart was telling him to do with his life. His soul showed him how to perceive his life differently so he could learn what he needed. Rich finally accepted his heart would guide him not only to a joyous life but also to a prosperous one.

For Rich, the session was pivotal. He cleared the reasons that prevented him from hearing his inner guidance and became acutely aware that he hadn't listened to his true Self for years. He listened to others, to his fears, and followed his old patterns but never stopped to listen to the small voice within whispering to him to ease up, relax, and enjoy life. The inner voice was buried because his heart was troubled. After the session, Rich felt considerably lighter and returned to Kansas a stronger person, committed to listening to his heart for inner guidance.

Recognizing Perfection

A primary purpose of a Heart Awakening session is to help you experience your Divine Self, free of all pain and suffering. From the perspective of spiritual healing, we are already whole and healed. We don't need fixing; we are simply releasing what isn't real to reveal what is. Heart Awakening helps you experience your own perfection, which is often enough for you to change your self-image completely.

In a session, many people are awestruck when they see themselves filled with light and their physical form as an emanation of light. This experience helps them recognize that, in their Divine essence, they are much more than a decaying body with irresolvable baggage. The eternal nature of who we are in our essence never goes away.

Betty was overweight. When she came in for a Heart Awakening session, she had learned to hate herself for being so heavy. Nothing she did to lose weight ever worked and she believed that she could never change. As a result, Betty wished she were dead.

During Betty's session, she experienced herself as whole, healed and perfect. In her Spirit personality she was not overweight at all. She didn't just imagine herself as being thin; she visually and energetically experienced herself in her Divine essence and saw she had always been whole. Indeed, her actual beauty and radiance stunned her.

After the session, Betty could never think of herself as the person reflected in the mirror. She saw her true Self, her true essence, as revealed by Spirit. Within a week, she had lost 15 pounds without really trying. Just the memory of the way she is in her perfection caused the change.

Realizing Your Source Of Creativity

Many people feel a connection with the Divine through prayer, meditation, or even the joyous interaction of a spontaneous social gathering where Spirit guides the moment. These are all part of a Heart Awakened life, yet what the sessions offer to both the giver and the receiver is an opportunity to give language to the Divine Grace underlying all creation. Divine Grace is experienced as a non-dualistic state. It is the process of making conscious the deep, inner wellspring of our true essence and bringing it forth into language. Each person has a way of expressing this connection in a unique way.

Jeanette had been a professional writer for many years and was currently writing a book for a particular spiritual teacher. She knew he had something. She couldn't quite figure out what it was, but her task was to write about it.

Jeanette decided to have a Heart Awakening session to help her understand the message of the spiritual teacher. What she experienced surprised her. The session helped her find her own inner Divinity when she felt the presence of her guides and teachers. Visions of her own future were revealed, including where her writing career was headed.

Once she discovered this place inside her, Jeanette knew it was the source of her creative writing experience. The essence of her heart contained the magical elixir to help her readers awaken to their own beauty. She melted with joy and felt the inevitability of her journey and its work. Most importantly, she made the jump that aligned her with what she was here to do on earth. There was no more doubting or looking for it on the outside - she had found it.

Jeanette finished the book for the spiritual teacher and moved into an exploration of her heart's script for a better life. Something in the grace and tenderness of the shift she experienced during her Heart Awakening session touched her forever. She made the connection, knew the purpose of her life, and now her writing would be an expression of divinity rather than an expression of the ego.

Expressing from Your Heart

On one level, everything we think, say, or do is a part of the Divine energy field. Yet what happens when we let go of thinking, live in the present moment, and allow our creative expression to flow?

The massive force and strength of pure Divine Love is overwhelming. Through Heart Awakening, we gradually learn how to express from this energy and feel its full effects flow through us.

When that happens, it is You speaking. Not the ego you; but Spirit from within. It is you at a much higher level of frequency. Heart Awakening is an experience of the greater Divine Self taking over and being a conduit for all that is. The ego is simply an observer and a witness to the expression.

As you allow the language of the Divine to be expressed through you, there may be a change in your voice. Traces of the ego are dispelled, and your voice carries a purity of tone and integrity free of judgment, blame, and the accumulated vibrations of your personality traits. It becomes solid and certain and carries with every word a massive power of Love that brings healing to any situation. It becomes rich and pure because the language and the wisdom expressed are of the higher Self and not the ego.

When Divine energy is expressed through language for the purpose of helping another into the heart, the Divine presence through Self can be experienced. The intent of the communication must be in keeping with what the Divine consciousness would want, for only then does it flow. The Divine consciousness asks us to love one another and be happy and from this place all else flows.

We believe in Love, yet only a tiny fraction of its potential has been expressed. Heart Awakening is an opportunity to go further into the language of pure, unconditional Love than ever possible in ordinary life. The articulation of our Divine Self brings with it the experience of heaven on earth when you surrender and allow yourself to feel compassion for another human being. Spirit works and supports such attempts in unfathomable ways. Even the slightest effort extended by the least knowing is supported by the infinite power of Divine Love, Divine power, and Divine wisdom when the intent is to help another into the heart.

All energies of a spiritual nature are perpetual and forever uplifting. Those of a physical nature are depleting and need constant replenishing. The doorway into perpetual energy is the present moment, for within it is contained all the information we need. You might not know how you know - the knowledge is simply there. These energies are available through the principle of service. The Divine consciousness needs form to grow, and Heart Awakening is a vehicle for that growth.

Your Heart Awakening Adventure

When we grow tired of the material world, it may be a sign that we are ready for a true adventure into the depths of our own soul. This adventure is one of the greatest gifts from a Heart Awakening session.

How far can I go? How deeply can I get into the sacredness of all that is within me? Is it reachable? What are the deep desires within me that have lain dormant and are seeking expression? Is there a voyage I can take to resolve the guilt and shame I carry and bring me back to the essence of all that I am? Did I

go wrong on my life's journey? Have others or I
caused the lessons I need to learn? Am I acting out
the family karma without realizing I haven't given
space for my spiritual nature? Who am I? What am
I? What am I made of? Is there more to life than the
humdrum superficiality of daily life?

These are questions to ask yourself in the search
for an awakened heart. Part of yourself can look at
the world and sense a deeper meaning behind everything and an awareness that things should be different. That part will guide you through the maze of
your own feelings back to the essence of what lies
within. The experience is not humdrum, nor can it
be obtained in ordinary life. The full impact of
knowing the true light of Self is perhaps the greatest
adventure anyone can embark on.

*Jeremy came to his session full of questions about his life and
identity. Although he was filled with joy and anticipation as
a boy, his sense of exhilaration and joy of life was buried under
a mountain of responsibilities and work over the years.*

*During his session, Jeremy expanded his consciousness to
open his mind and heart to a vision of Divine Magnificence.
A renewed sense of the intense joy and infinite potential of life
filled his entire being. In remembering the vastness and splen-
dor of Divine creation, Jeremy once again became infused with
the sense of adventure and anticipation that made his life
worth living.*

*When he returned home, Jeremy took his wife and children
on a trip to Alaska which renewed their sense of wonder for
life. It also gave them the time and space to deepen their bonds
of love and realize what was and was not important in life.*

Heart Awakening sessions are an opportunity to

listen to the voice of Spirit more clearly than ever before. You move beyond form and structure into a moment-to-moment revelation of what happens in the healing process when Spirit takes over. The sessions help you understand healing doesn't have to be created through a model or a specific line of questioning. Each session is an unfolding, a work of art, a unique act of creation and a release from the complexities of the outer mind and its fragmented analysis of what the healing process should be.

Sessions are a gift from Spirit for both the giver and the receiver as a reward for coming into full integrity. All we need is the willingness to step in that direction and Spirit does the rest. Eventually, each of us must cross this bridge.

How is the true essence of your Divine nature expressed? The Divine can come through in many ways - singing, sculpting, dancing - for it flows through everything all of the time. But Heart Awakening occurs when we want to give language to the Divine love within.

The gift of Heart Awakening is a wide-open heart and unlimited freedom. The result is unmistakable, for it shines through every particle of your aura. It is your body, your higher self and your divine self all functioning together. Once you go through a Heart Awakening, everyone you know becomes aware something in you has shifted. The truth of its presence is undeniable, even to the greatest skeptic, because you remember what you know you should remember. The energy of Spirit is certain, leaves no doubt and is the guiding light for which all of us are searching.

PART E
THE JOY OF YOUR HEART
AWAKENED LIFE

The Life of a Heart Awakener

The process of becoming a Heart Awakener
is a gradual commitment
to discovering the presence of God's love.
The path of a Heart Awakener
is a journey to finding the Divine
within all people, within all things –
most of all within oneself.

This is the gift of enlightenment.
It is seeing the light, seeing the Divinity
within everyone and everything.
This ongoing process is a spiritual path
and a spiritual journey in and of itself.

The commitment to being a Heart Awakener
is a commitment to completely dissolve
the needs, wants and desires of the ego.
Inherent within this commitment
is the knowingness that one
will be confronted with all the power and gifts
that reside within oneself.
The work and the path of the Heart Awakener
can move forward only when one's own
"stuff" has been handled.

The Heart Awakener's journey is equivalent
to the path that one has traveled
getting into one's heart,
because all of the knowledge gained

about how to get into one's own heart
is what is used to serve others.
The work of the Heart Awakener
begins to be feasible when the partnership
with the Divine has been earned.
This happens when sufficient spiritual practice,
prayer and meditation,
has been done so there is a *knowingness*
that what is asked for in prayer
can be received.

The moment this has actually become
a *fact* for the teacher/student,
is when the support, the guidance
and the assistance to manifest the path occurs.

This path is an expression
of one's connection with the Divine,
and the partnership with the Divine
must be there for it to be fulfilled.

Once the partnership has been established,
there is a learning curve based upon
the right use of that partnership.
When the teacher/student Heart Awakener
embarks upon the journey of helping others
reach the Divine within themselves
and be all they can be, without controlling,
without enabling, then energy can flow through.
Answers to prayers are heard and supported.

For a person who is committed
to being a Heart Awakener,
there is an incredible amount of support
for the work that comes from the higher realms,
from the Higher Self,
because there is in essence a commitment
to *bringing Divine Laws into tangible experience.*
This is the primary work to be done
on the planet at this time.
Becoming a Heart Awakener
is a commitment to heal oneself,
a commitment to being willing
to come into full integrity
with all areas of one's life.

It is a commitment to bring in
love and heart energy where there is conflict.
It is a commitment to maintaining
physical health and vitality.
It is a commitment to being literally
all that we can be.

Making the commitment
to becoming a Heart Awakener
is experiencing the greatest potential in
your life on Earth.

But when a path is set forward in life,
with the knowingness that its fulfillment
will heal your soul's desires,
then your life takes on

a much higher level of energy.

Simply by making the commitment,
there comes a willingness and a knowingness
that all suffering inside will dissolve.
So the commitment within itself
is a commitment to the expression
of the Heart Awakener's own wholeness.
And that very decision literally means
an end to all of the inner suffering,
in due course, in due time.

Even though the commitment has been made,
the ego will be seduced into many other things,
so there will be a constant learning.
The purpose of this will be a discerning
of what love is and what love is not –
and how the love flows through all that is,
all situations and all people.

It is the ongoing commitment
and experience of touching people
in their hearts
that allows the journey's path
to be paved in front.

The joy of helping someone
fully experience all they are, and
helping them set their spirit free,
provides rewards that are beyond description.
We see them on their life's track,

on their purpose,
based upon their own heart's desire
and their own connection with Spirit.

Perhaps one of the greatest gifts
of being a Heart Awakener
is actually being able to see
how love is forever present
in each and every situation and circumstance.

The challenge of the Heart Awakener
is to stay joyful, to continually let go
and stay in a state of trust,
forbearance and knowingness
that all will unfold perfectly –
simply by holding the knowing
of the inherent perfection within all things.
Indeed, that is the job.

This becomes a process of anchoring, saying:
"I know there is a Divine Perfection
manifesting itself through all of life.
I stand as a representative of that energy,
and I express myself from it.
I help others come to that same understanding
and that same awareness."

This is the life of a Heart Awakener.
And it is so.

CHAPTER 14

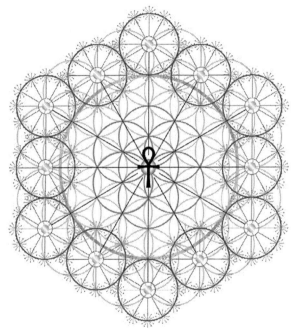

LIVING FROM
YOUR HEART

What makes Heart Awakening such a joy is that everyone is ready. Most of us long to return to our hearts, to allow the presence of Spirit to help us return to our precious space within. People are drawn to this work because they want to be empowered by co-creating with the Divine. With this strength, they can change and make their lives work.

People also come because of a genuine need for vision at this time of intense change. So much adapting and flexing is necessary we need a deeper sense of where we are going and what we are here to do. Heart Awakening is for those who genuinely want solutions to move forward.

Living in Abundance

An overriding reason why people are ready is that restoring the co-creative partnership with the Divine is essential to practical daily living. Whatever your career or situation, your capacity to know the Divine within and how to work with it forms the basis for manifesting your material needs. Many of us feel too entrenched in material needs to focus our time on developing a partnership with the Divine, yet that is what allows unlimited abundance to flow through our lives. The universe is naturally abundant and the notions of loss and scarcity are man-made concepts with no basis in truth. It isn't possible to solve a problem of scarcity by focusing on the outer world because true abundance must be accepted as an inner state of consciousness. Once this is done, the outer world will reflect the inner state.

When our feelings of shame, guilt, or fear are unresolved, it is harder for us to feel deserving of incredible abundance. Heart Awakening opens the energy of the heart and allows you to accept abundance as the natural order of the universe. Once accepted, abundance becomes a reality, taking the form you most need at the moment - friendships, romance, wisdom, money and more. It is the energy of the universe perpetually flowing through us, and within it is the Divine plan.

To develop a creative partnership with the Divine, you need to become conscious of the Divine plan for your life. Once realized and accepted, the partnership becomes the foundation for a genuine, spiritually based life. Heart Awakening gives you the opportunity to align with Divine energy and realize you are wanted, loved, and appreciated. It invites the deepening of the Divine partnership at all levels of your growth. As the heart opens, the outer mind realizes abundance is not a result of ego-striving but comes as a natural result of being re-aligned with the Divine reality in which all of our needs are met at all times in complete love. Living from the heart is like being in a miraculous world where everything has changed.

Tracy left a three-day Heart Awakening workshop fully centered in her heart, and was amazed at how the world had "miraculously" changed around her. Without any action on her part, people were much nicer to her and began bringing her gifts. Even the man at the gas station gave her a discount for no "apparent" reason.

She found her life started to click in a way she had never thought possible. A business deal she had been working on came together. For the first time, Tracy experienced how being in the flow of divine, heart-centered energy really worked. She completely let go, and the universe responded with her heart's desire. The world was no longer at fault and making her unhappy because her inner perceptions had shifted and her outer world now reflected the inner change.

Once Tracy reached the inner place where she was at peace with everything, she found her relationships also improved. For her, the gift was knowing she no longer had to "do it all herself." She no longer tried to make things happen and events began to unfold in ways much better than she ever imagined. Her boyfriend shifted a long-held difference of opinion, and they planned to live together. She still had to work to stay in her heart, but found it much easier once she experienced the results of letting go and trusting.

Living in Love

To live in your heart, it is essential to know how to convert negative emotional feelings into unconditional Love, and this cannot be done by the ego personality that has yet to commit to a path of unconditional love and healing.

Danny was a well-established, successful marketing consultant, never at a loss for words in his day-to-day life. During the energy portion of his Heart Awakening session, I found the core blockage of what he needed to resolve in his aura. In it was an ingrained habit of communicating to others solely from ego rather than from the heart.

When I simply asked him to speak, he couldn't and was stuck for two hours. All his normal faculties stopped functioning. He was at a loss. Danny gradually realized he had never truly spoken from his heart and, as a result, he had distanced and alienated himself from other people.

Eventually, Danny did speak from his heart; and the moment he did, Spirit gave him all the understanding he needed to express his love with his family. His heart burst open and he felt pure Divine bliss throughout all the cells of his body. In the energy he felt complete, whole, and secure, as if he had finally found the spiritual home for which he longed.

Spirit gave Danny an understanding of the co-creative partnership with the Divine that would unfold in his life. In learning how to speak and communicate from his heart, he was able to continue his career with a much greater appreciation of who he was and what was inside him.

Facing Challenges

Truly living in the heart can produce challenges because once Spirit shows the truth to us, it can no longer be ignored. One of the great strengths of Heart Awakening is to help people access the Divine Love within so they can complete difficult relationships of the past and live in their hearts.

Karen's Heart Awakening session focused on the real difficulties she had with her father. He was in the hospital, not expected to live much longer, but Karen could not accept his dying. Even as his condition worsened and her father expressed a need to resolve past differences, Karen's ego continued to ignore his need, saying "it will be all right."

During her session, Karen realized she was angry with her father for unfairly punishing her during her childhood. She never forgave him and that locked-up anger kept her from expressing her love to him.

The session helped Karen see her father as his Divine Self. She felt love for him flood through her body and was able to forgive him and herself. She accepted his impending transformation from the body, knowing it would release him from physical pain.

Now she was left with the task of visiting her father in the hospital to have a genuine, open, heart-to-heart communication with him. She was grateful for the opportunity to speak her truth, not in a hurtful way, but in a way that allowed the love to flow between them once more.

Karen was able to communicate with her father on a soul level and complete their relationship. In doing so, her father was set free of the bonds holding him on earth in sickness and pain and Karen was free to live life in her heart.

Committing to Heart-Centered Living

Committing to living from the heart means a life where the ego is no longer in the driver's seat, but rather lives in and surrenders to Divine Love and guidance. It can be a tremendous hurdle for people when they discover the ways of the ego simply don't work and they must begin to work with the deeper parts of themselves for their lives to have any real value.

Living from the heart means being all that you can be. Heart Awakening sessions bring the alignment and confidence necessary to restructure life on a much higher level of spiritual expression. They serve as a catalyst for major spiritual growth. This is the most critical need for mankind at this time - to uphold the natural sequential ordering of thoughts that come from the indwelling divine presence within self. The deepening of our ability to focus on our own presence opens the door to communication that contains our true selves - free from the past. Within the center of your being, you have the free will choice to communicate in the language of light love and power. This language is the language where true healing comes from. It comes from your heart, from your heart awakened state, where your real self lives. It is sometimes called the point of light within the mind of God. Willpower can be used to balance yourself in the heart mind body of your divine self. When we do this we can be free of controlling or being controlled by others. This brings the difference between the struggles of the personality self and the expression of the Divine nature into focus. The adjustment may take time; after all, it means you step into a whole new way of living and leave behind the old way.

People come from all over the world for sessions feeling their lives are in chaos and there's nothing left for them but work and more work. After a Heart Awakening, they discover everything in their lives was part of their Divine Plan and they just couldn't see it before.

Heart Awakening will change your life by bringing in the Love and understanding of the inherent benevolence in all life. Perfection is revealed. Once any situation is seen through the eyes of Spirit, it is impossible to hold onto judgment and separation. No thought, no pattern, no pain, no injustice can endure when Divine energies are brought into a healing session. The pain is over if you want to know peace and Love more than anything else in the world.

Completely seeing life through the energies of the heart is the same as going through life in an enlightened state. As we commit to living in the heart, we are conscious of the continual stream of Spirit's guidance telling us what to do even in the most precarious situations.

When the heart is open, solutions reveal themselves. The wisdom and power of grace allows these resolutions because Spirit knows everything about who you are, what you're doing, and what your motives are. Solutions that come from your higher Self are complete and serve everyone involved. You never have to wonder whether you did the right thing because the Divine energy moving through you helps you to where you need to go.

When the channel of communication is in place, an envelope of energy encircles the people involved. Through that envelope, Spirit's hand gently supports you, bringing forward ideas for the betterment of everyone. There are no mistakes because the conversation comes from the energy of the present moment. When Spirit's purpose is met, the energy dissolves and you know God's will was done. You realize you were part of something greater than yourself, yet it was you.

Let yourself be quiet and when you still the outer mind, you open up to the messages of Spirit coming in through the energy. You hear, see, feel, know, and recognize things for what they are and from where they come. They always energize and support the flow. All you need to do is relax and listen. The path of peace will be whispered to you. The path of

joy will unfold before you and the truth of your soul
will emerge triumphant. You will know the work
you came here to do - one step at a time.

Serving From Your Heart

Heart-centered service is given from the Divine
perspective, not a do-gooder mentality. It is a profound natural impulse to extend the energies of the
heart beyond yourself which is ultimately the path of
discovering your full essence.

As you step into heart-centered awareness, you
rejoice in opportunities to serve and are filled with
the mysterious presence of Spirit. Each time you
allow more of this presence to be felt, you set yourself
apart from the voices of doom in the world and
become part of the solution rather than part of the
problem. You recognize the only way to move forward is to deepen the experience of this Presence to
become all that you are. Spirit teaches you to move
in the direction of your true potential and the actualization of your true self. Each time you feel the presence of Spirit, you know it will take you to the ultimate fulfillment of your life's purpose. It is like
going on a ride where you can't fall off, so exhilarating you don't know if your heart can stand it, yet
your heart wants it. You have no choice but to go
forward, listening to the message your heart has been
carrying and recognizing this is what you came here
to express. It is your unique expression of service to
all life. As you release the potential of your heart's
song, you release God's plan for your path of service
and the healing of life, self and others.

All you need is to reconcile your relationship with the Divine and accept that partnership. What you give to it, it gives back to you. As a little child once again, you will grow with this partner in a circle of wisdom that will protect you for the rest of your life. It may be a long one, for the dance of Spirit continually regenerates the cells of your body, and there is much to explore.

The process of Heart Awakening is discovering heaven on earth. As your heart's journey flows, it reflects through you into the material plane where you demonstrate the possibility of its reality here and now. From the natural instincts of your soul, you align and flow with what is and become a part of bringing heaven to earth.

CHAPTER 15

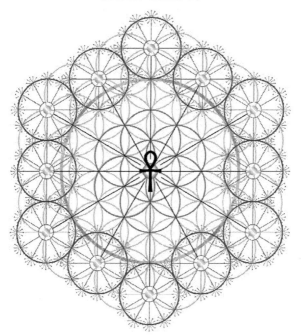

ACTUALIZING YOUR
TRUE SELF

R emember, 'energy follows thought.' Expressing thoughts about the nature of our Divine essence releases the unlimited amounts of Love within us. Sharing our thoughts reveals the nature of our essential selves to the world around us. Divine Love only knows how to share, expand, and grow. It cannot be contained.

Speaking from Your Heart

After people have gone through the inspirational transformation of a Heart Awakening session, they are simply more of who they are. Sessions help release the illusions that surround our true identities. Once shifted, being true to your heart is the key to actualizing your true self and your Spirit is free to shine forth.

Christine came for a Heart Awakening session simply because she had a feeling something was wrong with her life. On the surface she had a good marriage, a nice home, and a successful career in the cosmetics business. She couldn't identify what, but something was missing. The years kept slipping by with a deepening sense she should be doing something more with her life.

Christine's Heart Awakening session revealed how much her parents had loved her, but because she hadn't known how to express herself from her heart properly, she felt continually starved for love and affection from her parents. In their eagerness to make her happy, Christine's parents bought her expensive toys, took her on trips, and gave her everything money could buy. Because she never really communicated through her heart to her parents, they always had to second-guess her. Years later, Christine found herself with the same pattern of never enjoying heart-to-heart communication with anyone.

As she went through her session, Christine realized she used silence as a way to control her parents. This knowledge helped her accept a deeper level of responsibility about communicating her true feelings. Christine understood how she was being dishonest with others by never allowing them to know what she felt. She released the patterns from her consciousness and went through the feelings of guilt for the damage she was doing to herself in her relationships with others.

At first, she thought being in her heart meant giving vent to her emotional nature, but during her session she learned the difference between being emotional and expressing from the space of Divine Love within. When the "divine eye in me" sees the "divine eye in you" and visa versa, there is a shift of time and space into a non dualistic form of awareness that we call an awakening. The difference took her a while to put into practice, but the session helped Christine accept that the only real truth was expressed from her heart. She understood what she needed to do to actualize her true self in life.

Retrieving Your Spiritual Essence

When we retrieve the spiritual essence given to people and release situations that no longer serve us, we can reclaim the full and rightful use of our life-force energy. This is a key part of Heart Awakening.

Sometimes we feel as though we're going through the dark night of the soul where nothing seems to be going right and there is no end in sight. In truth, this is an offering of Spirit to let go completely and trust. It is an invitation to release a major life pattern and give birth to a whole new cycle of the soul's journey where the self can be actualized.

Over and over again, Heart Awakening sessions help people cross that bridge of uncertainty. We are here to discover the free will choice of the path to unconditional love and healing. The personality wants to plan and have its future securely organized, yet the voice of Spirit encourages people to live in the present moment and flow with all that is. This doesn't mean sitting, waiting, and doing nothing. It means placing our faith in the true Self rather than the outer self constructed by an ego personality that has yet to commit to a focus on unconditional love and healing – it is your life. Living or actualizing the path of the self comes as a result of listening, accepting and responding to the voice of Spirit that speaks through an open heart.

Louis had been a successful stockbroker for many years. Then, over a period of a few weeks he lost a large portion of his assets and his girlfriend abandoned him. He was in a deep state of depression, angry with himself, and had lost confidence in his ability as a stockbroker. He began to search beyond his usual sphere of existence for understanding.

As Louis' Heart Awakening session unfolded, his true Self admitted that for a long time he felt the stock market wasn't where his heart wanted to be. It was where Louis wanted his pocketbook to be, but his years in the business were eroding away a part of himself needing a clearer expression in a different form.

The session enabled Louis to make a deep connection

with his essence and place the affairs of the heart as his life's priority. He felt the emptiness of the life he was living, and yearned to be fulfilled spiritually by working with groups of people. He didn't know where this would take him, but felt his spirit soar at the prospect of exploring the possibilities.

Louis was able to appreciate his losses in the stock market and realized he wanted to lose the money because his heart wasn't in the right place. It took a great deal of courage to admit, but it was a truth that allowed him to move on and forgive himself. His joyous, childlike Self shone as a result. He reclaimed his capacity to listen on a much deeper level than ever before.

Louis put the life he had known behind him and reclaimed his energy for a new adventure of his spirit. When he let go of his position in the stock market, he entered a future of uncertainty. In the experience of his own essence, he knew fear would turn to faith, and following his heart would lead to receiving material abundance.

Realigning Your Career Path

It is highly rewarding to watch people make choices born of their hearts' desire. Perhaps the most rewarding aspect of a session is to feel the impact of someone's heart being fully opened, releasing old baggage that served no purpose and seeing the Divine nature shine through in spite of the accumulation of life's negativity. The full impact of experiencing the Divine Self has a profound, dramatic effect and transcends written description.

For many, the path of unconditional Love is the doorway to experiencing enormous amounts of joy and freedom. When Spirit moves through you, nothing is untouched and no part of you is forgotten. You feel freed in a way that gives you indescribable hope and passion. You are at peace, centered, and able to live the life you have always wanted because you know your true Self lives forever.

Peter's life was turned upside down. A sudden divorce left him not knowing which direction to take with his career. He weighed moving to Phoenix to be close to his children against staying in New York to look after his pharmaceutical business.

Peter's Heart Awakening session helped him clear the unresolved pain of being rejected by his wife. He accepted the fears that pushed her away, forgave himself, and found a clear space to decide what he really wanted from life.

Spirit did not give Peter the answers he expected. It seemed his soul intended to let go of the business and do something to develop a spiritual community. His soul was weary of the corporate treadmill and longed for a life of service.

Peter realized being true to his heart would make it easy for him to prosper and knew why he considered leaving his business and moving to Phoenix. His heart was moving him in a new direction.

Peter was grateful for the changes that occurred during his session. It showed him he could follow his heart and be himself outside the confines of a career choice. Three days later he received an offer to purchase his business. The universe confirmed it was time for him to move.

Your Life Purpose

It is important to follow the heart in any career

decision. Many times people change jobs because they make personality-based judgments about their work. Heart Awakening increases your understanding of your life purpose. Over and over again, the message is the same - to love, see life through the heart, abandon the old ways of the ego, and trust the Divine plan is unfolding and you are an intrinsic part of it. When you are in the flow of Divine Love, your purpose and God's purpose become one.

Nadine came in for a Heart Awakening session seeking her life's purpose. Preparing to leave her career as a nurse and embark on her soul's journey as a natural healer, she was exploring different healing modalities.

During her session, Nadine learned why finding her purpose in life had been so difficult. As a child, she was terrified of making a wrong career choice so she could never make up her mind what career would best allow her to actualize her true self. Her heart energies began to loosen and flow, and she realized her purpose was Love. Everyone was to be touched by her loving energy. It didn't matter if she was a nurse, a counselor, or a healer. Whenever she was in her heart and allowed the energy to flow through her, Nadine would know her purpose was being fulfilled. She thought she needed to know her purpose to open her heart, but the reverse was true. Opening her heart revealed all she needed to know about her life's purpose.

When Nadine saw her nursing job from the Divine perspective, she knew she had originally chosen it to serve, heal, and love others. Her purpose in life had been obscured because she was not seeing herself through the energies of the heart. She realized, as many others have, that our true life's purpose is to actualize the creative wisdom born in the heart. This is God's plan for us. Each time we open our hearts, the next step on the path to self-actualization reveals itself.

Quite surprised, Nadine decided to continue her nursing career to express the Divine plan for her life. Her desire was to open hearts, and Spirit revealed her nursing career was the best way to deepen her own capacity to Love. Knowing her purpose in life was simply to follow her heart filled her with a renewed childlike enthusiasm for life that made her glow from head to toe.

Nadine knew Spirit would continue to teach her how to heal through Love until she could have her own healing practice. In the meantime, she was grateful to see how spiritual healing skills could evolve through her present job.

CHAPTER 16

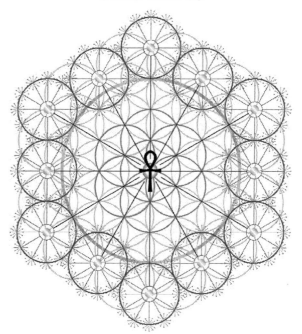

YOUR GIFT OF A HEART
AWAKENED LIFE

I embarked on the Heart Awakening journey because I wanted to learn how to love others, what that meant, and experience how deeply it could be felt. It was a choice my deeper Self knew would gradually correct the faulty perceptions I held of the world. This vehicle would enable me to forgive the past and do something worthwhile to help myself and others. Honoring myself and re-establishing a sense of self-worth based on my capacity to love and share, rather than on my capacity to make money and succeed in a personality-based sense, was challenging.

Developing Heart Awakening encouraged me to take prompt action and do what was necessary to restore my heart-centered awareness when issues surfaced. It was a way to align my personality in the proper direction, to build joy and find good in others even when they couldn't see it in themselves. It gave me a way to maintain my freedom, for the lifestyle that evolved from Heart Awakening was immensely inspiring and rewarding.

The greatest gift for me has been the astounding revelation of all the wondrous depths, nuances, beauty and immense complexity of our Divine selves. At one time in my life, I saw only the physical or outer manifestations of people as real. But within the revelation of heart-centered, awakened energies, I am able to perceive all life from the Divine perspective. I learned this gift is available to anyone and everyone who truly seeks to live in Divine Love and the energies of the heart.

Your Voice of Love

Learning to listen to the voice of love is one of the great gifts of Heart Awakening that opens the door to the path of actualization of your true self. Every moment we have a choice. We can listen to the voice of love or follow the voice of fear.

When listening to the voice of love, what you have to deal with is knowing your problems will suddenly be over. That is what people fear—finding themselves without their favorite problems to keep them occupied. So they choose not to listen. Yet each moment presents us with an opportunity to expand or to contract. When we listen to the voice of fear, we contract, believing it will give us solutions. Yet it is the voice of love that speaks of prosperity, abundance and the expansion of your true worth that will bring you peace and a growing sense of confidence about where to go and what to do.

The deeper Self knows the way forward, yet the outer mind in its fear would freeze the motion, needing to know a direction to feel safe. Spirit, not the ego, directs motion. If we let go of the fear that we are somehow going in the wrong direction, Spirit will move us exactly where we need to go. All we need is the willingness to learn to trust and have faith in Divine perfection.

Listening to Your Inner Voice

Guidance from your inner voice is one of the great gifts of a heart-centered life. Realigning with energies of the heart will be a step-by-step process of clearing past patterns and painful associations. But with perseverance and pure intent to live in the heart, the voice of your inner self will again be heard.

Be still for a moment. Listen inside. Do you hear the whisper that angels bring into your awareness, inviting you to discover how easy and natural this is? Take a moment and go inside. Reclaim your capacity to listen. The true voice is loud. Let yourself hear it, express it, and act on what you have heard.

What is being offered will melt your heart. It will change your life. You won't want to go back because you will remember just how easy it was all meant to be. The voice inside will guide you to prosperity and what you need to know and do. It cannot do this for you, but it can express through you. It can guide you, lecture you, snap you out of your fantasies, and set you on the road to recovery.

The choice is no more difficult than any other. It will free your time, your energy, and let you go where you need to go. You can choose to act on it and let your life change.

When you allow such an opening, the scattered energies re-form and assemble for their directions and re-assemble for their next adventure into Godliness. There is a path laid out before you, created for you by You. It accepts and enhances everything you need; it knows what is a part of it and what is not. Your task is to articulate it and follow it. The purpose of your life is to enjoy it.

Step into the present moment and flow with the energies of the Divine contained within that moment. You are, have been and always will be connected to this Divine energy. As you allow yourself to relax into your connection, you grow more conscious of the energy of the present moment. This is the real energy you seek, and its abundance is available to you.

This opens communication with Spirit guides and tells you where to go and what to do. Within the energy, no words are necessary. You get up when you need to get up and go places because it is time to go. When you are in the energy there is no longer any need to make decisions because you are conscious of the decisions that Spirit reveals.

Sometimes you might try to figure out, "What am I doing here?" The logical mind says you should be here or there. However, once you recognize you are always in the flow of Divine energy, you can see that Spirit provides the motion—all you have to do is stay connected with the energy. Then, allowing the motion to flow as you consciously move with the energy, you will discover what your attention is being drawn to. Allow Spirit to lead you. When you see what Spirit has been hoping for you to see, complete solutions appear, followed by a further surge of energy to take you in the appropriate direction.

Following the energy brings you the miracles you need. Material processes are secondary. They are there and attended to, but in trust and detachment come the tremendous gifts of communion with the Divine. You can't go anywhere without it, for you are never apart from it.

If you recoil from a sense of unworthiness, Spirit honors your not being ready and waits until you understand that you are a divine being, that you were born in the spiritual world, not the physical, and that all good things are your divine birthright as a part of the divine plan from which you are never separated.

Once you open to Spirit, you are like a fountain pouring out abundant goodness everywhere you go. The outer mind cannot handle what emanates from you, so it tries to muddy the waters, hoping the brightness won't reveal itself, yet the personality is constantly washed in the fountain, being cleansed and purified. No matter how much you cloak yourself in pain and sorrow, your goodness continues to shine brightly. Spirit within is far more subtle and powerful than you can imagine.

So this is the path of Heart Awakening - the capacity to release fear, to listen to the inner voice, to see beyond what is not, to what is, and to flow with the energy along the path to our true home within the heart of God.

YOUR INVITATION

A NEW BEGINNING

Where is your heart? What is it telling you right now? Can you remember the quiet vows you made to yourself before coming to this world, the ones you reinforced as a child? Do you remember those vows contained promises you wanted to fulfill? Do you recall being filled with conviction they would happen? Do you remember your sense of adventure and willingness for this to be true? Perhaps social conditioning and negligence have buried the message. But inside, in the energy of your true Self, there are certain things you know you are here to accomplish. I invite you to sit back, relax, and allow these memories to be revealed.

If you listen to these imprints unfolding your destiny, you can come home. Only a portion of your soul is here with you on earth. Most of your soul has always resided in the heaven worlds, and the link to your consciousness is always present. Listening helps you remember and align, and heaven on earth becomes a living reality.

You haven't been abandoned in a desolate wasteland. You are simply in the process of strengthening your connection to the Divine to bring back the memory of what you are here to do. You were promised you would be supported in every conceivable way, and you are.

If you don't know where to begin the heart-awakened journey, ask. If you don't know what to ask, request to be shown. A whole set of new options will be opened to you. Those possibilities will move you past the part of yourself that wants to remain static. What you seek is the motion, like flowing with the current on a river. What you need is in the motion waiting for you to experience it.

All of this occurs with your commitment to serve and your understanding that the true Self replaces all perceptions of imperfection. A boundless force of unconditional Love and infinite wisdom flows through everything. Everywhere you go, whatever you do, it is always present. The joy of living a Heart Awakened life is knowing that it opens the doorway to the perception of this force, which in turn deepens the Love. The joy of Heart Awakening is discovering and revealing the truth that Spirit is waiting for you beneath the chaos created by the outer mind. Knowing this truth is part of the ongoing discovery that the paths of Love bring all the magnificent rewards Spirit has to offer. The choice is yours.

Spirit simply asks you to not be attached to anything, because being attached is like anchoring yourself on one piece of the riverbank. The village of opportunity where you stop may have much to offer, but there are a myriad of villages further downstream beckoning the adventurer within you.

When was the last time you were able to reclaim all your spiritual power and direct it toward a single aim of the heart? Ask yourself, "Who am I, and what am I here to do? Where do I go? What do I say and to whom?" The voice of eternalness will gently answer, and it might surprise you because it is familiar. You will discover the voice of God and yours are one; that what you say can replace your ego, that you can become your Self, and the gentle power of Spirit will speak through you.

Be gentle and compassionate with yourself. Be still within yourself, and you will hear a heartbeat created by your Divine Self. In this heartbeat, the pulse of all your soul's desires exist, and everything is given to you. Will you accept an invitation to a path filled with joy? Spirit wants you to know the joy already exists within you. True joy, born of appreciating the goodness in life, fills your awareness when you understand everything you desire comes in letting go of all that is not Love.

Spirit wants you to lead a life between being and becoming. You keep on growing and moving forward, while at the same time relaxing and letting go. The motion Spirit intends reveals itself to you. Your foot becomes sure as the information flowing through you breaks down patterns of the past and the molecules in your body open to release the Divine consciousness within you. All you need is the willingness for the Divine light to shine deeply into every part of you and accept it within.

A Heart Awakening is a prayer for you to be all you ever wanted and experience it within. What more can you ask but the opening of the doorway into your Divine and perfect self?

Angels of Love surround you. Ask them to stand by you to give you the strength, the courage, and the wisdom to reveal the gifts along the path of unconditional Love. They will assist and guide you to Love so you can love yourself as totally and unconditionally as God loves you.

Heart Awakening offers an opportunity to rediscover a forgotten part of yourself. You will find the real you and this is the greatest gift you could ever give yourself. Open the doorway to self love and discover a new life of eternal joy within. Rediscover yourself as one within the Heart, Mind and Soul of God. May each of your hearts be filled with the Divine Love and peace that will forever set your soul free.

HEART AWAKENING SERVICES

Consciousness of Light is a spiritual and educational organization in Cave Creek, Arizona. It offers a wide range of services by spiritual healers with extensive experience in Heart Awakening and other modalities to help people achieve and maintain a Heart Awakened life. In addition to private Heart Awakening sessions, the wide variety of educational programs offered are designed to bring spiritual wisdom into practical daily living. Consciousness of Light also offers customized healing programs. Arrangements will be made for anyone living out of the area who is interested in receiving a Heart Awakening to host a Weekend in the Heart workshop. In addition, you can order audio cassettes, videos, and other products.

The School of Healing offers a series of courses for those who want to develop their spiritual healing gifts and become Certified Heart Awakening Practitioners. These courses are also offered on an individual basis for people to progress at their own pace. The faculty is led by founder Raoult Bertrand and consists of extraordinary teachers and internationally known healers in disciplines that synergistically supplement the Heart Awakening approach. The school also offers an intensive teacher training program for Certified Heart Awakening Practitioners who want to express their commitment to serve humanity by teaching the Heart Awakening process to others. The School of Healing also offers 5-day healing sessions for those who want to rejuvenate their spirit and reconnect with their purpose in life.

"Every adjective you can imagine falls short of capturing what Heart Awakening has to offer. Years of other self-improvement therapies, including psychotherapy, body work and spiritual practices have not accomplished what was achieved in a single three-hour session. Having been seriously ill for most of my life, I have tried every kind of health and spiritual healing known to man for more than thirty years. To my astonishment, the immense power and profundity of a Heart Awakening swept away within a few hours a mountain of mental, emotional, and physical pain and trauma. Speaking from years of experience, there is nothing on Earth that compares to a Heart Awakening." -M.C.

"Heart Awakening's capacity to help an individual restore the ability to Love Self makes this an essential piece of the healing puzzle." -C.F.

"For 'truth' to be true, it must set the heart free."
-R.B.

CONTACTING US

Call   1-800-370-5479 or 480-488-1731
Fax   480-488-5806
E-mail: contact@ConsciousnessofLight.com
Website: www.ConsciousnessofLight.com

I need the following info:

_____

_____

_____

_____

_____

_____

Fill out and return to:
P.O. Box 4195, Cave Creek AZ 85327

Please send me:
_____Newsletter_____School catalog
_____Put me on your mailing list

Name_____

Address_____

City_____State____Zip_____

Telephone_____

Email_____

Website_____